My Year in France

Wartime Memoir & Diary
of Harlem Hell Fighter
Sgt. Clinton J. Peterson

With Over 90 illustrations

I0167960

Edited by
Richard Sears Walling

Communipaw Group
July 2019
© All Rights Reserved

ISBN-13: 978-0-9768719-4-1

Citation for Croix de Guerre
First Sergeant Peterson, Clinton J.
104315

1st Sergt. Peterson, at dusk, on Sept. 26th, 1918, in Ripont, still under heavy machine gun fire, remained under this fire, attending to the wounded and utilizing the slightly wounded to evacuate those more seriously wounded. Continuously, and again at the Village of Sechault, by his example and under heavy shell fire, he reorganized the remainder of the Company, going about from man to man, taking the names of those present with pad, and pencil; disregarding the cautions of all to seek cover.

"Nor will I forget the bravery of my loyal Sergeants, Clinton J. Peterson, Herman Brown, and William Layton, who carried out their duty to the men under heavy shelling at great risk to themselves. At the end of World War I, I told my men, 'You have fought and died for freedom and democracy. Now, you should go back home to the United States and continue to fight for your own freedom and democracy.' "

Hamilton Fish, III
Memoir of an American Patriot, 1991

"Evening World" February 8, 1919
New York's Black Watch Lauded by French General

2 November, 1918

Le Colonel Hayward, Cdt. le 369 Regt. d'Infie, U.S.:

My Dear Colonel – I am greatly pleased with your thoughtful attention. You have collected the water of the Rhine in your hand and you have placed the "Black Watch" along the river.

It is ours from now on, but no Frenchman ignores that it is to the Americans that we owe this conquest. Therefore, you will permit me not to accept the personal compliments you paid, except with the following reserve: I shall never forget that the opportunity has been given me, in the course of this war, to have under my command an American regiment which, with little previous training, has fought with extreme bravery, and, which since the last combat has applied itself to such regular and steady work that as far as attitude and military discipline are concerned, this American regiment can compare with any of my French regiments.

Therefore, it is to yourself, Colonel, to Lieut. Pickering and to your battalion commanders that must be addressed all our congratulations. And, it is for this reason that I make it a point to reward officially the 369th R.I.U.S. with a collective citation in the orders of my division.

When the citation is approved, I shall have great joy in decorating your flag and in kissing you in front of your regiment. And that day, we shall not only drink water from the Rhine, we shall drink champagne, and it will be a beautiful day for your General commanding the division.

Believe, my dear Colonel, in my sentiments of affection and comradeship.

G. Le Bouc

General, commanding the 16th French Division.

Dedicated to George Alonzo Sears (1894-1962)
My grandfather who served during World War One.

Knew him when I was a child – left behind dead soldiers in
our garage after a summer of painting our house.

Glad you made it home!

TABLE OF CONTENTS

This is a work of non-fiction, based on the memoirs and diary of Sgt. Clinton J. Peterson. For further information, please contact the author at richwalling@hotmail.com. For more information on the famed Harlem Hell Fighters, see *From Harlem to Hell and Back* on Facebook.

Foreword

This is a story of a black American hero, born in the last decade of the 19th century, who rose by his own hard work and initiative from the depths of poverty to the solid middle-class. Clinton Jerome Peterson was the living embodiment of the quintesential Horatio Alger story, a truly American tale.

Clinton was born on June 7, 1891 in the wooded hills of Kent, Putnam County, New York. The last of eleven children, his father Jeremiah (aka John) was seventy-five when he was born and his mother, Nancy, was in her late forties. In 1900, only two other siblings remained, and the elderly parents and eight-year old Clinton were inmates of the Putnam County Almshouse, along with about thirty other people of varying backgrounds and ages.

Father Jeremiah (also John in records) had been born in Belvidere, Warren County, New Jersey, in the Delaware Valley, about ten miles north of Easton, Pennsylvania. We don't know of his life there, but he was born in about 1816, just after the War of 1812 and forty-five years before the American Civil War. He married Nancy Higgins and at some point moved to Putnam County, which straddles the eastern shore of the Hudson River, across from Bear Mountain and West Point. Due to their poverty, John and Nancy put their older children out to work. By 1900, eight of the children were dead and the elderly parents and young Clinton were the wards of Putnam County. Shortly after the turn of the new century, Jeremiah Peterson died. Mother and child drifted from place to place, eaking out a life as best they could. They boarded at various places, including Marlboro, a small community five miles north of Newburgh, exchaning chores for a place to stay and meals. Clinton attended schools as best he could as they moved about, and finished grammar school up to the sixth grade. By 1910, he was a chauffeur and handyman for a woman in Kent, and he and his mother were living in Kent Cliffs where he attended the Baptist church there.

It should be noted that his parents lived in a place that was predominatnly white and Protestant. This may lead some to conclude they were looked down upon and the subject of discrimination. Those assumptions would be wrong. Clinton was active in the church and was a member of the youth group there. As regards to their economic status, they were certainly not alone. The rough hills of Putnam County of 1900 were little different from when the first settlers arrived. Industry was limited to nearby towns like Peekskill and Poughkeepsie, and the wild hills still resonated with the names of the Algonquin-speaking Wappingers who had lived there just a handful of generations before.

In 1900, according to census records, there were two hundred forty-nine families in the Town of Kent; of that number, there was one black family and three individuals of that race spread amongst its forty-three-plus square miles. In nearby Carmel, home to the Putnam County Courier weekly newspaper, there were six hundred and forty two families, only three of which were African-American, and one of those was a bi-racial marriage consisting of an Irish man married to a younger black woman native to New York State. Of the William and Nancy Thomline family, the three very young children were identified as black in the census. The Town of Carmel consisted of a core village, dating to before the American Revolution, and a large rural area. Carmel could count twenty-one single African-American men and women, most of whom were recent arrivals from Virginia and North Carolina who had moved north in the years leading up to the new century. These individuals were laborers and servants, and even a coachman, illustrating the continued rural character of the community at the time. The hamlet of Carmel was five miles distant from Kent Cliffs, in a scenic valley of reservoirs fed by the west branch of the Croton River.

At age twenty-five, Peterson volunarily enlisted in the newly-created Fifteenth New York Infantry, Colored. This was a National Guard regiment formed as a result of strong lobbying from the emerging African-American community in New York City, with the backing of Republican Governor, Charles Whitman. Authorized in 1913, it took three years of hard work (including overcoming US Army resistance), and the border crisis with Mexico and Pancho Villa, to finally see the birth of the regiment in 1916.

It is said that war makes a man. If true, it is a terrible crucible to endure to reach personal self-actualization. Peterson saw his duty clearly; he enlisted out of patriotism shortly after the United States declared war on Germany, and his maturity, clear-headedness and innate intelligence ensured his success in the military. There was only one caveat to consider – would he survive the horrific battlefields of the Western Front, with its millions of casualties already soaking French soil red with blood?

Finally, before we let Sergeant Peterson tell his story in his own words, we must acknowlege one other major player in this tale: Hamilton Fish, Jr. (III). A Harvard graduate and athlete, heir to a Hudson Valley political dynasty, mirroring his neighbor Franklin D. Roosevelt, who lived nearby at Hyde Park, Fish was the company commander of Sergeant Peterson. They suffered together in the trenches of France and shared the same dangers and experiences, and although of opposite extremes of both economic and social orders, they were comrades-in-arms, brothers born of war. Fish's story adds details to Peterson's, and so, there is an Appendix filled with wartime letters from Fish that will help to tell a more complete story of Sergeant, later Major, Clinton Jerome Peterson.

Special thanks to Rick Soedler, site manager of the Brinkerhoff House, East Fishkill Historical Society (EFHS), Bill Jeffway of the Dutchess County Historical Society, and to Jen McCreery of the Fish-Desmond Library in Garrison, New York. Among the noted historians of the 369th, and to whom a great debt of gratitude is given, are Jeffrey T. Sammons, Ph.D., and author Stephen Harris. Finally, a very special note of regard to Major General Nathaniel James, of the 369th Historical Society. The General is representative of all the men and women who cherish the record and memory of the regiment. Through the efforts of all these individuals and the 369th Historical Society, the story of the Harlem Hell Fighters will never be forgotten. Mr. Alan Leibson also lent his substantial editorial talents to this project.

A note on sources: The text presented in this work are the words of Sgt. Peterson. Editorial annotations are from the 1920 report of the regimental history of the 369th Infantry, available at the New York State Department of Military Affairs website. Hamilton Fish letters are at the New York State Archives.

Pictures and maps come from a variety of sources, all available on the Internet. In particular, special mention is given to *Camp Dix News* (1917); *Complete History of the Colored Soldiers of the World War* (1919), written by a number of African American vets, including Sgt. James Jamieson of the 369th; *History and Achievements of the Fort Sheridan Officers Training Camps* (1920) and *Gold Star Honor Roll: A Record of Indiana Men and Women Who Died in the Service of the United States & Allied Nations in the World War* (1921); the National Archives photography collection; *93[d] Division Summry of Operations in the World War* (1944); and, the 1937 federal government's series on the US Army's wartime record, American Expeditionary Forces, Vol 1.

Special recognition to Fulton Search, an astonishing compilation of American newspapers brought togetgher in one location by Tom Tryniski of Fulton, New York. It is the dedication of individuals such as Mr. Tryniski that our history is made readily available to the world.

Richard Sears Walling
June 2019

Peterson Plans for Memoir

Fresh from the battlefields of France, Sergeant Peterson arrived home on February 2, 1919 aboard the ship *LaFrance*, along with the Third Battalion of the 369th United States Regiment of Infantry, the federal designation for the 15th New York National Guard.

His arrival home was heralded by the local newspaper on February 7, 1919 (Appendix Four), and his community was overjoyed by the return of their hometown hero:

> Sgt. Peterson enlisted in the old 15th Infantry, N.Y.N.G., when it was being recruited and was a member of the company of which Hamilton Fish, Jr., was Captain. He has remained with Capt. Fish's company throughout the war and the regiment is now the 369th Infantry... It is expected that Sgt. Peterson will soon return to this country and his many friends are anxiously waiting to greet him.

Sergeant Peterson was a celebrity. During the next several months, the newly discharged warrior was a much sought-after speaker at various community groups and churches. For example, on April 9th, his own congregation hosted a special event in his honor:

> The Baptist church at Kent Cliffs held a patriotic meeting on Tuesday evening. The program consisted of an opening selection, "America," prayer by Rev. A Christensen, of Troy, N.Y., a former pastor; solo "Long, Long Trail," by Rev. A. Christensen, and a speech by Sergeant Clinton J. Peterson, during which he exhibited some relics of the world war and described the use of various articles that are part of the equipment of a solider in the United States Army. Sergeant Peterson then told some of the experiences of army life; camp, transportation, and the trenches, very

vividly describing a scene of "no man's land" during an attack.

Never the man to let an opportunity escape his grasp, and to further cement his status as a hometown hero, Sergeant Peterson undertook the hard work of putting into words his military experience to be published in serial fashion for the Putnam County Courier. Beginning on April 11, 1919, just two months after his return home from overseas, and ending in August, Peterson wrote nineteen articles for the paper. The Courier was a small, weekly publication, with very limited subscription; Peterson devoted his energy to telling his story, fresh from the battlefield, as it were.

His was not the only effort to tell the story of combat veterans in general, and of the special circumstances of the some 400,000 African-American servicemen who served in France (about 23,000 saw combat, the remainder were assigned as Service and Supply troops). Sergeant James A. Jamieson of the old 15th, along with other black non-commissioned officers, for example, wrote *The Complete History of the Colored Soldiers in the World War* in 1919.

W.E.B. DuBois, a vocal leader of the NAACP and editor of its magazine, *The Crisis*, was eager to tell the story of the war from the African-American perspective. At the behest of the NAACP, which strove to both document and tell the story of black soldiers, DuBois published in the March, 1919 issue of *The Crisis*, a brief article "The Black Man in the Revolution of 1914–1918." Calls for information appeared in the magazine, and veterans began to send him their stories. Peterson responded positively and willingly shared his own set of clippings from the Putnam County Courier with DuBois:

Letter to W.E.B. DuBois of the NAACP - 1920

115 So. James St.
Peekskill, N.Y.

Aug. 2, 1920
Mr. W.E.B. DuBois
70 Fifth Ave.
New York, N.Y.

My dear Sir;

Replying to your letter of the 29th ult. will say that I will be able to let you see a copy of "My Year in France" which was run as a serial in a local weekly.

I will mail same to you within the next three days. I will also say that the story as it appeared in the paper is not at all the way I would wish it to appear in book form.

It was written without care or preparation, the evening before it had to be in the office I would sit down and hurriedly write enough to fill the space allotted to it. It was written in long hand and in many cases when it was not too legible it was set up wrong which resulted in a meaningless paragraph. Besides many parts of it are of only local interest. I have been promised the aid of several of the officers of the regiment in writing the story for publication in book form and I shall be able to secure many photographs and other matter of interest for the purpose but being busy and also believing that it is better to wait until the market is less flooded with work of this kind I have done nothing in regards to it.

In mailing you the story I do so trusting that you will return same as I am not at all sure that I can secure all the back numbers.

Should you care to know more of me I would ask that you call at Col. Hayward's office at 120 Broadway and Mr. David A. L'Esperance who formerly commanded 3rd Batt, 15th N.Y. Inf. N.G. can tell you of my character or, Major Hamilton Fish, 115 Broadway, who is personally acquainted with me both as a soldier and civilian both of whom will lend assistance in the writing of this story.

Very Truly Yours
Clinton J. Peterson

P.S. Old address Garrison, Putnam Co. N.Y.

Time went by with no word from Mr. DuBois, whose vision of an all-encompassing volume on the experiences of African-Americans during the war, and the broader implications for dark-skinned races then under colonial rule in Africa and elsewhere, stalled. The on-line article, "World War I in the Historical Imagination of W.E.B. Du Bois," provides an in-depth account of his role in telling the story, but suffice it to say, his goal was not achieved. Other books on these topics were published, and DuBois had chronicled some of his information as articles in *The Crisis*. His plan for his own publication went unfulfilled, but Peterson did not know that. Nearly a year-and-a-half after giving DuBois his personal collection of newspaper clippings, he was becoming anxious about his ability to tell his story to more than just a few hundred people in Putnam County:

Letter to W.E.B. DuBois, 1922

Source: W.E.B. DuBois Papers, UMassAmherst.

In October 1920 I sent you newspaper clippings of a story "My Year in France" which at that time I considered have published in book form. I have not heard anything more from you in regards to these clippings nor your own history of "The Negro in the World War."

One month later, DuBois personally wrote back:

Feb. 20, 1922

Mr. Clinton J. Peterson
P.O. R.F.D. 3.
Peekskill, New York

My dear Sir:
    I have still your material here. I am hoping to finish my manuscript this spring and will then return all of the material which I have. My book will be published, I trust, before fall.

Very sincerely yours,
[W.E.B. DuBois]

The fall of 1922 came and went with no further publication from DuBois, and apparently Sergeant Peterson's only copies of his epic were never returned. His intent to publish his own war story, complete with graphics and input from his officers, went unfulfilled. His career, both professionally and militarily may have distracted Sergeant Peterson from the mental exercise of trying to re-tell what had come so (relatively) easily to him in early 1919.

His story, "My Year in France," follows. It is the only account of its length and detail published to-date by a member of the famed Harlem Hell Fighters. His diary, written between November 1917 and May 1918, is also included – although badly compromised by the hungry little mouths of insects. Details are rounded out by letters written by Peterson, articles about his life and activities, and by the words of his commanding officer, neighbor, and friend, Captain Hamilton Fish, Jr. (III). Sergeant Peterson's intent was to both inspire and enlighten his fellow Americans – it is the editor's hope that those objectives will be fulfilled.

PART ONE

"Putnam County Courier" April 4, 1919
Sgt. Peterson's Story of the War Starts Next Week
Kent Cliffs Boy to Write "My Year in France"

Next Friday, April 11, the <u>Courier</u> will publish the first installment of Sgt. Clinton J. Peterson's own story of the war, entitled, "My Year in France." This will be a vivid and accurate account of the life of Sgt. Peterson, of Kent Cliffs, during the trying days he spent facing the Huns in the front line trenches.

Sgt. Peterson's story will be published in installments and will cover a period of about three months. The number of copies of the paper are limited to the orders received so that persons desiring this story should place their orders at once. A three-months subscription to the paper, which will cover the complete story, is 50 cents.

The following short biographical sketch of Sgt. Peterson is given:

Sgt. Clinton J. Peterson was 25 years old when he enlisted in the 15th New York Regiment (Colored) on May 12, 1917. He spent some time at Camp Whitman in Dutchess county and also at the Peekskill state camp in Westchester County. He was at Camp Dix in New Jersey and later was sent to Camp Wadsworth. He sailed on Nov. 12, 1917, for France, but a breakage of engines in the ship caused the boat to return to port and on Dec. 2, 1917, he embarked again. He arrived in France on Dec. 28, 1917.

On August 1, 1917, he was made a corporal, and on Sept. 1, 1917 a sergeant; on Mar. 1, 1918, a supply sergeant and on Sept. 12, 1918, first sergeant.

During his service in France he spent 191 days stationed in front line trenches. He participated in a German raid on June 12, 1918; in the German offensive, July 14-July 20, 1918; and in the French offensive Sept. 26-Oct. 2, 1918.

He sailed from France on Feb. 2, 1919, and was given his honorable discharge from Camp Upton on Feb. 22d, 1919.

Sgt. Peterson was soldier No. 104,315 and his discharge bears the following:

"1st Sgt. Peterson has at all times since his volunteering, proven himself a man of the highest ideals, most sincere devotion to duty and capabilities. His conduct in action is shown by his receipt of the Croix de Guerre given on Jan. 9. 1919."

Camp Smith, Peekskill, NY 1917
Capt. Hamilton Fish, Jr. left center
Courtesy of the Desmond-Fish Library, Garrison, NY.

INTRODUCTION*

Knowing that everyone has been more or less interested in the recent war and anxious to hear as much possible about it from someone who has been "over there," has prompted me to write this article.

There will be, in the very near future, many good books by able writers, which will give, with the aid of photographs, a very good idea of the various ways and means by which the great conflict was brought to a victorious end, giving figures that would drive a mathematician or statistician into convulsions, but as most of these will come from the pen of those who have never been beyond Divisional Headquarters, they will not be able to tell the feelings and thoughts of one who goes out on patrol, working party or raid on a cloudy night, to have a "star shell light" from the enemy lines disclose his position and half a dozen machine guns begin sending their messengers of death irritably close to him, at the rate of 500 shots per minute, and you wish that, instead of having hands on the ends of your arms, you were equipped with steam shovels so that you might "dig in," or while standing all night in the front line positions waiting for the "zero" hour and the command, "Over the top," where you know you must either kill or be killed.

Before starting my story, I wish to make all due apologies for grammatical errors and claim exemption from criticism in that respect as I am neither student nor writer, but am giving my plain story of the war in plain language.

A few introductory remarks will, I think, help the reader to understand the story better. While my experience differs, no doubt, from that of soldiers of any other regiment in the minor details, such as going for 4 days without a change of socks (though no fault of those in charge of that department, but because of conditions brought on by battle) for instance, it is as a whole practically the same as that of anyone else, who has spent a few months in the first

Italicized text is information added by the editor of this book.

line trenches, dodging bullets, ducking shells, putting on and taking off gas masks to keep the poisonous gasses from the lungs and evading the hundred and one other humane (so called) methods the treacherous Hun has of putting one's name on the "casualty list" or "honor roll."

My regiment, the 369th United States (Colored) Infantry, which came to be better known as the "Hell Fighters," was formerly the 15th New York Infantry National Guard, and was organized in the summer of 1916 by Colonel William Hayward, former Public Service Commissioner of New York City.

Capt. Hamilton Fish, Jr. with members of Company K – the unit he raised in the lower Hudson River Valley, including Clinton J. Peterson of Kent.

On May 13, 1917, it was ordered to State Camp, Peekskill, N.Y., by former Governor Whitman for target practice and maneuvers, remaining there until May 31, 1917, when it was dismissed. In a letter from the President of the village to the Commanding Officer, it was stated that the orderly conduct and discipline of the members of the regiment while stationed there exceeded that of any other organization that had ever camped there prior to that time. It was the first regiment of the N.Y. National Guard to reach war strength, when it became known that all units would be called into Federal service on July 15, 1917, the next closest being the old 69th N.Y. Infantry, N.G.

19

Instead of training as nearly all of the militia did after being Federalized, it was ordered to do guard duty and was divided into small detachments and sent to various parts of New York, New Jersey and Pennsylvania, where it did excellent work until it was again assembled in October. After a 12 day stay at Camp Wadsworth, Spartanburg, S.C., it was ordered north to prepare for immediate sailing. On Nov. 12, 1917, the regiment embarked on the U.S. Pocahontas, sailing the same night but was forced to come back the following day as one of the engines broke and the ship was unable to keep up with the convoy. After many difficulties, it finally embarked December 12, 1917.

It was the second regiment of New York to go to France, following closely the 69th Regiment of the Rainbow Division, and was among the first 100,000 "over there," arriving December 1917.

When the regiment represented one-hundredth part of the American Expeditionary Forces, it was holding one-twentieth part of the front held by United States troops.

It was the farthest east of any American troops at the signing of the armistice and, singularly enough, the farthest north of the old 69th, which had been so closely associated with us in so many of our achievements.

It has the distinction of being the first American troops to gaze upon the Rhine, as well as having the honor of carrying the first American flag to wave over the most beautiful of rivers, when the triumphant Allied armies marched forward into the reclaimed territories to the German border, following closely upon the heels of the disheartened and demoralized German army, the remnants of what was one of the world's greatest military organizations, as they slumped away into the interior of their Fatherland, and were lost to view in the dense undergrowth on the opposite bank of the Rhine. It had grown from lack of attention since they had come forth a little over four years before, with their new uniforms, bands playing and heads erect, hoping to conquer the world.

Lest some of my tales should be looked upon with doubt and my ability as custodian of the truth questioned, I will give a few figures to show that everyone is not killed because they happen to spend a few months in the front lines.

Statistics from the Allied armies at the close of 3 years war, which ended August 1917 (when Americans began making their first appearance in the trenches) showed that about 6 ½ percent were killed, about 10 percent were permanently disabled and between 25 and 30 percent were wounded, who returned to the lines within six months.

These figures were quite as consoling to the soldier when he started for the front as for the relatives whom he left and he enjoyed himself a great deal more than he would had he known that 30 per cent of an army never goes to the front, but it engaged in the various duties that are necessary to maintain the fighting men at the front.

Many times, though the doughboy (Infantry man), as he is dodging death at the front, wonders why he could not have been fortunate enough to have secured a position "back in the S.O.S.," (Service of Supplies), as it is called, when he thinks of the very quiet and pleasant life they must lead back there, with nothing to worry them except an occasional bad cold or the sad news that it will be impossible for them to get a 48 hour pass for the week-end.

Members of the 15th NY arrive at Camp Dix, August 13, 1917.

ARMY LIFE

While my story is of the life on the other side, I will give the reader a little idea of what the soldier finds on this side as he leaves his home and goes step-by-step towards "No Man's Land."

My experience is along similar lines (minor luxuries) and is intended to show some of the things that every soldier experiences, when he first enters the service.

The Regular Army man enlists for a stated period of active service with a stated period of reserve, and upon enlistment is given a few weeks drilling in what is known as the awkward squad, until he can do the various movements without being shown or told. He is then assigned to a regiment which contains men whose length of service may vary from a few weeks to many years. He has shown, by offering his services, that he is willing to suffer the hardships that at times are the soldier's lot. These men are the first to go in the field in case of hostilities.

The National Guardsman enlists for a stated period of active service and a stated reserve, but does not give his entire time to military instruction. He drills one or two nights each week and spends a couple of weeks each year in camp. He has shown by enlisting in this branch that he does not care to give his entire time, unless necessary, but is willing to be trained, so that, in case of war he can be of almost immediate service, needing only a final polishing to be ready for the enemy.

During the reserve enlistment, a man can be called without conscription, but is under no military obligation except if war is declared and men are needed at once.

The National Army man is entirely different. He was taken for the duration of war from all walks of life, from the farm to the office, and, although his treatment and achievements "over there" were just the same as all others, before he went there he had to be broken in until he could stand the severe tests that soldiers in actual battle are subjected to.

America's Record Since Entering the War Two Years Ago

A Few of the Statistics Relating to Our Armed Forces, Casualties, Shipping, and Estimated Cost of Operations, April 6, 1917, to April 6, 1919.

April 6, 1917—

Regular Army	127,588
National Guard in Federal service	80,456
Reserve corps in service	4,000
Total of soldiers	212,034
Personnel of Navy	65,777
Marine Corps	15,625
Total armed forces	293,438

Nov. 11, 1918—

Army	3,764,000
Navy	497,030
Marine Corps	15,627
Total armed forces	4,333,047

Soldiers transported overseas	2,053,347
American troops in action, Nov. 11, 1918	1,338,169
Soldiers in camps in the United States, Nov. 11, 1918	1,700,000
Casualties, Army and Marine Corps, A. E. F.	282,311
Death rate per thousand, A. E. F.	.057
German prisoners taken	44,000
Americans decorated by French, British, Belgian, and Italian armies, about	10,000
Number of men registered and classified under selective service law	23,700,000
Cost of thirty-two National Army cantonments and National Guard camps	$179,629,497
Students enrolled in 500 S. A. T. C. camps	170,000
Officers commissioned from training camps (exclusive of universities &c.)	80,000
Women engaged in Government war industries	2,000,000

Behind the Battle Lines.

Railway locomotives sent to France	967

Freight cars sent to France	13,174
Locomotives of foreign origin operated by A. E. F.	350
Cars of foreign origin operated by A. E. F.	973
Miles of standard gauge track laid in France	843
Warehouses, approximate area in square feet	23,000,000
Motor vehicles shipped to France	110,000

Arms and Ammunition.

Persons employed in about 8,000 ordance plants in U. S. at signing of armistice	4,000,000
Shoulder rifles made during war	2,500,000
Rounds of small arms ammunition	2,879,148,000
Machine guns and automatic rifles	181,662
High explosive shells	4,250,000
Gas Shells	500,000
Shrapnel	7,250,000
Gas masks, extra canisters, and horse masks	8,500,000

Navy and Merchant Shipping.

Warships at beginning of war	197
Warships at end of war	2,003
Small boats built	800
Submarine chasers built	355
Merchant ships armed	2,500
Naval bases in European waters and the Azores	54
Shipbuilding yards (merchant marine) increased from 61 to more than 200.	
Shipbuilding ways increased from 235 to more than 1,000.	
Ships delivered to Shipping Board by end of 1918	592
Deadweight tonnage of ships delivered	3,423,495

Finances of the War.

Total cost, approximately	$24,520,000,000
Credits to eleven nations	8,541,657,000
Raised by taxation in 1918	3,594,000,000
Raised by Liberty Loans	14,000,000,000
War Savings Stamps to November, 1918	834,253,000
War relief gifts, estimated	4,000,000,000

The National Army man is entirely different. He was taken for the duration of war from all walks of life, from the farm to the office, and, although his treatment and achievements "over there" were just the same as all others, before he went there he had to be broken in until he could stand the severe tests that soldiers in actual battle are subjected to.

Immediately upon the declaration of war in April, 1917, the United States began forming plans for getting her fighters in the field and early in June the first contingent of this country arrived in France and began making preparations for the great numbers that were to follow. These men were of the Regular Army.

On July 15, 1917, all State militias were mobilized and sent to camps to have their final polishing up and to be mustered into Federal service. These men began going over early in the autumn, immediately behind the "regulars," and were the National Guardsmen.

23

On September 19, 1917, the first men were called to the various cantonments for training and followed the "guardsmen" across except for a few Quartermaster Corps that did not require any special training, as their work consists of handling the supplies that the fighting man requires. These men are what is known as the National Army.

The men of the National Army enjoyed one privilege that was denied both the "regulars" and "militias." While they were escorted from local boards to railroad depots with blaring bands and cheering crowds, after beautiful feasts, the others were moved about silently by night and loaded on transports camouflaged by darkness, the instruments of their own bands cased and not even allowed to whisper as they silently moved out of harbor.

On the other hand, however, these fellows probably felt worse with all this ceremony than the fellow who was stolen away, because of the fact that the average person thinks war and death are synonymous and the tears which came in the eyes of relatives, as they waved a last good-bye to their loved ones when the train moved away, left such an impression upon the would-be-hero that he had a constant dread and fear of something until the armistice was signed and he knew hostilities had ceased.

These little groups as they left the local boards would proceed to some point and there meeting others would be consolidated and sent in detachments of several hundred to the designated cantonment.

These cantonments had been prepared with great thoughtfulness and contained every convenience that money and short time would permit. The buildings which are called "barracks" (meaning a hut or house for soldiers) are about 60 ft. x 140 ft., are well lighted and aired, are two story, have two large rooms on each floor, are sealed with wallboard and have a large heater in each room. Sanitary toilets and bathrooms are generously provided, so that no one need go without a bath.

The soldiers have spring cots with mattresses and, with electric plants and sewerage systems in each camp that would make many city officials hang their heads with shame, the embryo soldier finds himself in such congenial surroundings that his spirits begin to rise and he wonders if he wasn't a bit mistaken in his hasty conception of army life.

He arrives in the camp in civilian clothes covered with dust, after having marched from the station behind hundreds like himself, looking curiously at all his new surroundings and the many soldiers he sees, some drilling, some working, some playing but all apparently enjoying themselves. They are all taken to Camp Headquarters and checked, and are then divided up in small detachments and turned over to guides who take them to barracks where they rest until they get some food.

Nothing is done the first day. If they arrive in the morning, they have much longer to rest before the next morning and their new life really begins. If they arrive late at night they have less. Whichever it is, that night as they lie down they try to draw a picture of "No Man's Land" and, between that and the thoughts of what lies ahead of them on the morrow, they fall asleep.

Meanwhile, at Camp Headquarters, everybody is swearing because these new men have come, as they must have various rosters prepared before morning and various blanks must have each man's name typewritten on it, so that they may be quickly examined, clothed and equipped with all the paraphernalia that goes to make up what Uncle Sam calls "heavy marching orders."

The embryo soldier is dreaming, perhaps, of the "girl he left behind," who kissed him so affectionately at the station that morning as he left. He is returning to his hometown once more, after four years of war and hardships, and is calling upon the one he knows will be his, because of the promise she made that morning as he was leaving. He has a German helmet that he took from off the head of one of those killed and which he thinks would make her a beautiful flower pot. As he approaches the house, he thinks he will look in the window to see if he can still recognize her, as she was only 18 when he left and he has been gone so long. He sees her, yes, and seated upon the lap of some fellow whom he does not know. Infuriated, he rings the bell and, as he does so, he is awakened by someone who pulls the blankets off him and says, "Get up, and fall in.: It is the sergeant, and he gets up and falls in with all the other fellows of that barrack for roll call.

After roll call, they are marched to breakfast and then they go to the Medical Department where they are examined and if O.K., are taken to another building where they are asked about a thousand questions. The one that is best remembered is, "Who shall we notify in an emergency?" After all official papers are made out, they are then "sworn in," a proceeding that takes little time but which means a great deal.

The next thing is the uniform, which everybody is anxious to get and which nearly everybody is as anxious to get rid of when the war is over. These proceedings sometimes cover a period of two or three days and occasionally is done in one day. The soldier does not do anything though, until he gets his uniform. The blankets, mess kit, knife, fork, spoon and cup are usually issued before any other equipment so that troops will have something to eat from and sleep on.

After the above articles have been issued the soldier begins his training.

After the solider gets his uniform, he is soon started at the intensive training that is necessary, in order that he may be on an equal footing with his adversary when he meets him, and this training is, in most cases, continued until he will do the various things in the prescribed manner, under any conditions that may arise; and I can assure the readers that some of them are such as would cause the average lady to, at least, faint.

For the first few days, he is drilled in what is known as "close order" drill, which is largely for discipline and to instruct troops in moving in various kinds of formations. Except for the discipline it produces it is of no use on the battle field, but, no matter how well soldiers may have fought, they would receive little applause if, when parading before the large crowds, they moved as a mob instead of a well-regulated machine; hence the several days or weeks of hard work, that to the soldiers seems to be wasted time, money and energy. However, I have seen soldiers come on the line in replacement detachments who, 30 days before had been civilians and who knew absolutely nothing about warfare.

Early Rising in Camp

The soldier is awakened at 5:30 a.m. (the schedule of calls varies at each camp, but this is a good example, and the hours given are the usual ones for starting and ending the soldier's day) when "First Call" sounds. Reveille is sounded 10 minutes later and at that time he supposed to be fully dressed, bunk made up, and standing in line to answer "roll call," which is completed by each company's First Sergeant by 5:45, at which time he reports the number present, absent, etc., to Company Commander!

The next 15 minutes are devoted to "setting up" exercises, which put the muscles in good shape for the duties of the day.

He is then dismissed and goes to wash up, if he did not have time before reveille. At 6:15, "Fatigue Call" is sounded and all men not sick must get busy to thoroughly police camp, picking up the smallest piece of paper or scraps that are thrown about each day.

Disposal of the Sick

"Sick Call" is by 6:20 and all who are sick report to the "infirmary" in charge of an "N.C.O." (non-commissioned officer), who has their names written on the "sick book," a small book with blanks for names, disposition of the case, etc. Each company has its own book and each company is attended separately. The surgeon takes the book and calls the names, when the man answer "Here," step up and tell their troubles. He examines them and marks the disposition of the case according to seriousness. "Hospital" means that the man will be sent to the infirmary, "quarters" means that he must remain in his quarters and in bed, "light duty" means that the man should keep fairly quiet, perhaps a little police work, or peeling potatoes in the kitchen; "duty" means that the man is well and available for anything.

In the army, men figure every way to get out of doing anything and the "sick book" gag is almost as bad as the small boy's dead grandmother on the day of the big leagues play in town. Not wishing to do much on an especially hot day, the soldier gets a "Be Your Own Doctor" book and, after studying the symptoms of some disease until he can say it forwards or backwards, he falls in line for sick report and, if can fool the surgeon, he will lie in the shade all day. The surgeons know this and, as a result, they become very skeptical when the percentage of sick in a company is very high. The result is that, often times, a really sick man is marked "duty."

A very large amount of iodine is used in the army and the following story will tell the reader how quickly it is thought of by soldiers when anything goes wrong.

A soldier was walking along a road in France when he came upon a Lieutenant of the Medical Corps laboring with a Ford, which had utterly refused to advance. He had exhausted all his mechanical knowledge and he asked the young chap if he knew anything about automobiles. He replied that he did.

The M.D. asked him what he should do. "Well," replied the lad, "If I were you, I'd paint the damned thing with iodine and mark it "duty."

Routine of Camp Life

"Mess call" is at 6:30 and I will add here that that is the first call the "rookie" learns.

"First call" for drill at 7:20 is followed by "assembly" in 10 minutes. At first call, everybody "falls in" and at assembly, the first Sergeant reports to the C.C. (Company Commander) the number of absentees with causes for absences. Everyone must be there except those on special detail or excused by reason of sickness.

"Recall," at 11:30, ends the morning period.

The next half hour is spent in rest or in any way pleasing to the men until "mess call" at 12:00.

The afternoon drill schedule is usually from 1:30 to 5:00 and is followed by "retreat," which is at various times, but usually around 5:30.

At retreat, the colors are taken down and the soldiers stand at "present arms," if in formation, or at "salute," if not, while the band plays the "Star Spangled Banner" and the colors are taken down.

After supper, which is at 6:00, the men are free to wander about the camp, visit the Y.M.C.A. or any of the various places that are about the camp for the amusement of troops. At 8:30, "tattoo" is blown and is a signal for all soldiers to start for their regimental area. At 9:15 or 9:40, "call to quarters" is sounded and is the signal to get in your tent or barrack and is followed by "taps," 15 minutes later. This schedule or a similar one is maintained by soldiers at all times, except at the front, and on Sunday, when drill is omitted and "reveille" is a little later.

Overseas Equipment of Solder

At the end of a week or 10 days the soldier is issued a rifle and then begins his instruction in its use. At first it seems very heavy to him (weighs about 8 1/2 pounds), but by constant practice he gets so he can handle it with as much ease as the bookkeeper, his pencil. More attention is paid to bayonet exercise than target practice, and all troops who fight with the rifle are well able to defend themselves in a hand-to-hand encounter with the enemy.

When the first American troops went abroad, they did not receive their helmets or gas masks until they arrived in France, but later it was found that they could carry them and thereby save room for freight as no more space is needed for a soldier with gas mask and helmet than without. Great attention is paid to gas masks, and all soldiers must become efficient in quickly adjusting them before they can go to the front.

The intensive training is kept up until sailing orders are received, then daily inspection follow until the men finally embark. When the soldier embarks, he must have the specified equipment and so each day it is inspected and all shortages filled. The following list shows what each soldier has issued to him by the government and if, at an inspection, any article is missing, it is immediately supplied and charged to him and deducted on the next pay roll.

> 1 O.D. coat, 1 pr. O.D. breeches, 2 O.D. shirts, 2 suits underwear, 4 pairs socks, 1 overcoat, 1 pair gloves, 1 waist belt, 1 pair leggings, 1 slicker, 2 pairs shoes, 4 pairs shoe strings, 1 service hat, 1 hat cord, 2 collar ornaments, 1 razor, 1 shaving brush, 1 tooth brush, 1 clothes brush, 1 tooth paste, 1 shaving soap, 1 comb, 2 towels, 2 boxes shoe dubbin, 3 blankets, 1 shelter half tent, 1 shelter half tent pole, 5 shelter half tent pins, 1 condiment can, 1 bacon can, 1 meat can, 1 canteen, 1 canteen cover, 1 knife, 1 fork, 1 spoon, 1 cup, 1 rifle, 1 rifle sling, 1 bayonet, 1 bayonet scabbard, 1 cartridge belt, 1 pack, 1 pack carrier, 1 haversack, 1 first aid packet and pouch, 1 entrenching tool and carrier, 1 helmet, 1 gas mask, 2 identification tags and tape.

If in addition to this the soldier wishes to carry a few personal articles (excluding outside wearing apparel), he may do so, but it is a rare thing to see anybody with more, as this becomes very heavy toward the end of an all-day march.

System of Embarkation

Organizations going overseas are sent to one of the embarkation camps which are close to the ports, and from there they are taken to the transport.

The system of loading is excellent and it is a simple matter to load from three to five thousand troops aboard one of the transports in half a day, assigning each man a bunk and lifeboat. As each man steps up the gangplank, he is given a ticket showing which deck he is located on, the number of his bunk and the number of his lifeboat. Down in the hold of the ship are rows of bunks, three tiers, and just enough space enough between each row for a man to pass. Each bunk is numbered and he only has to find the deck, and then hunt a short time to find his number. As soon as he has gotten his equipment off, he goes up on deck and finds the location of his lifeboat, so that he will be able to get there without delay in case of need.

Sgt. Peterson and Company K were stationed at Camp Dix, New Jersey, for several weeks during August and early September 1917 as camp guards. Several of his letters from this posting are included in Appendix One. In mid-September, the Second and Third Battalions of the 15th New York National Guard were sent along with other New York National Guard units for further training at Camp Wadsworth, near Spartanburg, South Carolina. Southern customs and culture were not welcoming to black men from northern states. Several incidents occurred at Spartanburg which nearly resulted in violence. After a mere twelve days in the Deep South, the US War Department found it best to ship this unit as quickly as possible to France. However, it was an "orphan" regiment, not a part of a larger brigade or division. It shipped out in November 1917, but a series of misfortunes caused the ship to return to home port twice. Finally, the USS Pocahontas left Hoboken on December 12, 1917, and arrived off the coast of France at the end of the month.

WHERE BROADWAY COPS MAY HAVE TAKEN A LESSON

AROUND THE 15th BAND STAND
Source: Camp Dix Pictorial Review, November 1917.

SHIPPING OUT

The Trip Across

The trip to Europe, as the American army took it, was not what one would call a pleasure trip. Men are packed in the ships like sardines in a box and the air becomes very foul at night when all the men are below. All matches, cigars and cigarette lighters are taken away from the men and it is strictly forbidden to smoke, except on deck, and then only between sunrise and sunset. The throwing overboard of anything, no matter how small, is forbidden, and failure to obey these rules will put the offenders in the "brig."

Photo # NH 82957 Troops on USS Pocahontas

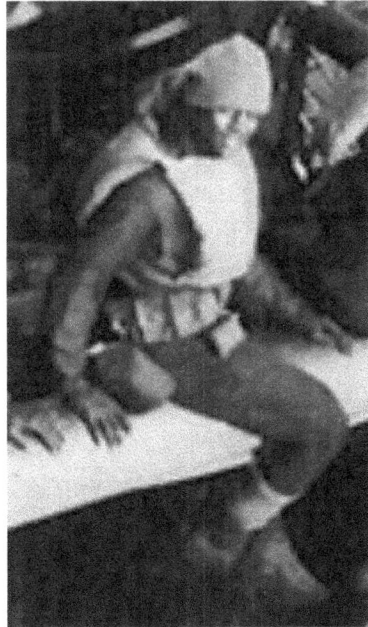

These images of the *USS Pocahontas* were taken in 1917, showing the 15th NY NG aboard.

The brig is a small, stuffy, unlighted room where those confined get a very little food, if the guard happens to think of it, and where one might easily be forgotten in case the ship was torpedoed. The room, which is rarely ever larger than eight feet by eight feet, is absolutely bare, except for the metal walls that enclose it, and those who get in once rarely ever do anything that causes them to be put in again.

These transports usually leave harbor as soon as it gets dark and travel without lights. The following morning they have the first "abandon ship" drill, and, as the bugle sounds, everyone except those on duty, who have been told that there would be a drill, rushes to their places on the deck from which the lifeboats are launched. It is so planned that each board carries a certain number of the ship's crew and at least one of the army officers to command the soldiers.

Everyone wears a life belt day and night and never moves without a full canteen of water, and it is quite amusing to see the troops rush up on deck when the call is given. These calls are never ignored, as no one knows whether it is drill or reality. The food aboard a transport is usually better than the soldier is accustomed to and in this respect he is filled with regret at leaving the ship when they yell, "France, all off."

The ships do not travel alone, but usually in groups of five or six, guarded by a naval fighter, usually a cruiser, which goes as far as the war zone and then turns back, after being picked up by the French convoy, which is composed of from three to six torpedo boats destroyers.

As the soldier gets his bearings aboard ship, he begins to get friendly with the sailors and, if he happens to become acquainted with one, he soon starts asking him all sorts of questions about the other side; how many trips has he made, if he has seen any "U" boats, what France looks like, where the soldiers go when they leave the ships, etc., etc., etc.

A very sharp "look out" is maintained during the entire voyage for submarines and the gun crews practice daily, as well as spend a little time each trip at target practice.

The commander of the ship that I went across on (*U.S.S. Pocahontas*) stated that if no one lost his head the last man to leave the ship could do so within twenty minutes and, if torpedoed, it would take at least thirteen minutes to sink.

Photo # NH 82958   USS Pocahontas in camouflage, during World War 1

As the ships glide into the harbors on the other side, women and children come out in rowboats begging for money, food and souvenirs from "Amerique," as they call it, and our boys at once begin to "parlez Francaise," it being their first opportunity to find out if anyone can understand them. It is quite amusing to see an American soldier, who has studied soldier's French and never heard a word spoken, except as he or his comrades have done it, try to make the French understand him. Because they cannot, he is apt to draw the conclusion that they are awfully dumb. After being on the restless sea for a week or more and then seeing a strange city filled with strange people who speak a strange language, but is on terra firma, he at once makes up his pack and anxiously awaits orders to debark so that he may see all the men and interesting sights.

OVER THERE – ARRIVAL AT BREST

The sea voyage is very tiring, especially to troops, as they are so crowded that they were not able to get sufficient exercise and, when land is sighted, everyone feels much better; they breath freer because they know the submarine danger is over and they are uneasy until they are on good old terra firma again. My regiment landed at Brest, after being at sea eighteen days, and, when land was sighted about 9:30 a.m. on the morning of Dec. 28, 1917, everyone tried to get on deck to have a look. We were sighted from shore at about the same time and two aeroplanes came out and looked us over to see if we were friend or foe and hovered above for a couple of hours. The harbor at Brest is very shallow and, as we steamed in, they kept sounding so that we would not get aground and it was not until 2:30 p.m. that we finally anchored about one-half mile off shore. There are no piers to accommodate the large vessels and consequently they have to anchor out in the harbor. From there the troops and freight are loaded onto smaller boats and taken ashore. As we lay in the harbor that afternoon, women and children came out in small boats begging for money, tobacco and souvenirs, and everyone who had anything in this line began throwing it to them.

First Impressions

Everything seemed strange. The people [at the seaside came out in] small boats. [They were calling out to us] and were poorly dressed and looked very funny in their wooden shoes. The language was new to us and no one could tell whether they were wishing us good or bad luck, except by the expression on their faces, and by this it was easy to see that they were glad to have us come and help shoulder the weight they had been under a little over three years. Although the ground was covered with about a foot of snow when we lifted anchor on this side, the grass was green and the weather mild, over there.

Smaller boats had to offload from the larger ship, *Pocahontas*.

The city looked a great deal different from any American town I have ever seen. The buildings are nearly all built of concrete, finished white, and with roofs of red tile, they present a very beautiful appearance. There is an occasional stone building, but one could travel many days in some parts of France and not see a wooden structure.

There are no skyscrapers and a five-story building is considered very high. As one goes inland, he sees villages with no building higher that one story and many with thatched roofs.

I was taken sick with mumps on board ship the day of our arrival and was taken off the same night and spent three weeks at Naval Base Hospital No. 1 [Brest] before rejoining my regiment at St. Nazaire. The regiment did not leave the ship for a couple of days, as it was necessary for them to get transportation before debarking.

Welcomed by the French

The morning that they were to leave, everyone was ordered up early and, after making packs, began cleaning the ship and then, as the small boars came out, they were taken ashore in groups of about

200. There they remained until the entire regiment was off. In the meantime, the French people began flocking around, as these were the first American colored fighters that had been seen and it seemed as if the entire city of Brest had turned out. When the band started playing and the regiment moved forward, everyone went wild and our boys were glad that they had gone over. This one scene was enough to repay them for the sacrifice they had made.

As they marched along, on both sides of the streets, stood young and old dressed in mourning, and tears ran down their cheeks as they recalled the day when their sons or husbands had gone forth with bands playing and flags flying and who are now sleeping "Somewhere in France." It is a pretty hard matter to find a family in France who has not lost someone in this war, and black is the color most seen on the streets.

As you go along the streets, you observe that nearly every other door is a café and the signs:

	BIERE	
VIN ROUGE		VIN BLANC

announces you will be able to get beer, red or white wine inside.

Traveling by Rail

If troops go to the camps at Brest, they have a three-mile hike up hill to the muddiest spot on earth. My regiment entrained upon debarking and went to St. Nazaire. As you approach the railroad station, on a siding, you see a long line of freight cars quite unlike those in this country.

They are about 22 or 24 feet long and each car has four wheels. These wheels are not solid, but have spokes, and are much higher than ours.

The coupling, too, is a little different as the cars are hooked together and, after being hooked, are tightened by a screw. On the ends of each are two large irons that have a flat face, about twelve inches in diameter, and are directly over the rails. These are held by springs that eliminate the jar when starting and stopping. Some have brakes, some have not, and, when a train is made up, cars with brakes are put in at proper intervals and men ride on the outside of these cars to operate them, which has to be done quite often, as the grades are terrible in some places.

On the outside of each car is marked:

HOMMES – 40
CHEVEAUX - 8

which means the car will hold either forty persons or eight horses. This can be done, but when troops get in them for a three day ride, about twenty less would make it possible for all to sleep at night. With forty in a car, they must sleep in relays, as all cannot lie down at once. There are no lights and it reminds one of a cattle train very much.

Our men were counted off in groups of forty each and quickly loaded. About 2:00 p.m., or 14 hours, the train started. The French have no a.m. and p.m. as they start at midnight and run to 24 hours the following midnight: For example, 18H20 means 6:20 p.m., 5H:40 means 5:40 a.m. etc.

Some of the cars had straw in them, and these were very comfortable. Others had no straw and became as cold as an ice box when the train got under way, the air coming in through cracks two and three inches wide in some cases.

When the regiment arrived in St. Nazaire the following morning, everyone was cold and hungry and about thirty percent had frost bitten feet and could hardly walk.

They were marched about two miles above the city to Camp N. 1 – Base Section No. 1 where they were fed late in the afternoon and given barracks.

1. CAMP NO. 1., St-NAZAIRE, FRANCE - At the close of the world war, 1919

Living in Barracks

These barracks were much different from those previously described. They are one story, about 18 feet wide and 100 feet long, without floors. A very small stove is located at each end and each morning you draw a certain allowance of coal which is about enough to last eight hours. The other sixteen, you freeze. The bunks are built by taking four uprights, seven feet long, and nailing four more on them about two and one-half feet from the bottom and four more near the top. Then strips are nailed through the center of each and chicken wire stretched across to form bunks for four men. About one hundred men sleep in a barrack and, if it is very cold, they frequently freeze.

We remained at St. Nazaire about a month, working at Montoir (pronounced Mon-twa) about five miles distant.

For the benefit of any soldier who has since been there, I will say that at that time we were filling it in with sand hauled from the ocean by railroad. I am told that there is a camp, which will accommodate 30,000 soldiers, on what was a worthless swamp in January, 1918.

Initiated in Use of Money

Here we began learning to parley Francaise, count francs and continue to get accustomed to the ways of the French people.

The French money is very confusing until you get used to it and you usually pay for your experience. The French had already found out that the Americans had plenty of money and, accordingly, had planned ways and means of getting most of it. The American soldier receives about $1.00 per day, while the French soldier gets five cents, except when at the front, and the French soon arranged things so that the Frenchman had as good a time for his day's work as the American.

The stores have three prices, namely; one for the Frenchman, one for the man who speaks French, and one for the man who does not speak French. It is needless to say that the latter is about double that of the Frenchman.

Where we measure the value in dollars and cents, the French have francs and centimes.

Their approximate equivalent is as follows:

French	American
½ centime	1 mill
5 centimes or 1 sou	1 cent
1 franc	20 cents
5 francs	1 dollar

They have 5, 10, 25 and 50 centime pieces; 1, 2 and 5 franc pieces. Each territory issues 50 centimes, 1 and 2 franc bills, which are good only within the territory. The Bank of France issues bills of 5, 10, 20, 50, 100, 500 and 1000 franc denomination and are good anywhere in France. They are not printed on good paper as our money and our men destroyed a great deal of it, as they would crumple it up and put it in their pocket. Do that once and the money is gone the same as any ordinary paper. The French all carry large bill books and fold only the large bills.

The bills are larger according to denomination, the smallest being the 5 franc note, which is about 3x4 ½ inches, and the largest, the 1000 franc note, about 7x10 inches.

Upon our arrival in France, the soldier goes to a Y.M.C.A. and gets his dollars and cents changed for francs and centimes and goes forth upon his first shopping expedition. If he was a fellow who drank and went over in 1917, he had no difficulty in getting a bottle of champagne for from 3 ½ to 5 francs; if he was one of the last, he would be lucky to get it for 20 francs, so great was the increase in price as soon as the French found the American was a good spender. I have paid 8 ½ francs for a No. 2 can of apple jam, which was nothing but applesauce with very little sugar in it. Eggs were from 15 to 20 cents apiece and hard to get at any price. Nothing is wasted over there and the average American family throws away enough food to maintain a family of the warring nations, who have been brought face to face with starvation.

The French are very slow going and one never sees anyone in a hurry. Everybody works that is old enough, and the women and children do all the work on the farm and in the town. Every man and all boys, who were able to shoulder a gun, did so and one never saw a man on the street, except in uniform, unless he had been disabled and discharged.

Poor System of Sanitation

The cities and villages are not models for cleanliness and one wonders why everyone has not died from typhoid fever long ago. There are no sewers and all filth runs down the side of the street.

There are no farm houses as in this country. You see a small village here and another couple of miles down the road. The house and barn is always under one roof and the house and barn door are side by side with manure heaps in front of both.

There are no fences between farms and when the cattle go out to pasture, a herder, who is usually a very old man, goes out with his dog and stays until it is time to return in the evening. Nearly everyone wears wooden shoes and the noise, produced by a lot of school children, playing tag on the pavements, is deafening.

We were at St. Nazaire about three weeks when, on night, an order came through for my battalion to prepare for moving at once, as we were to go to the interior of France.

Starting for Camp
February 21, 1918

My battalion fell in on the parade ground immediately after dinner, for inspection by the Colonel preparatory to our leaving. As soon as the battalion had been inspected, the Colonel gave us a few words of advice as to how we should conduct ourselves until we should assemble again.

The fife and drum corps of our regiment escorted us to the railroad station playing popular airs which brought the French people out to the streets where they cheered us as we passed and waved good-bye.

Who knows what the thoughts of these people were as we passed in under the long shed at the station and boarded the train? They had been doing this to Allied troops since August, 1914, and had never welcomed any back.

What thoughts go through the mind of the soldier as he marches along and sees this great crowd; old men, children and women; and realizes that he will not come back until the war is over, no matter how long it may take. I will not describe mine.

Colonel Hayward, playing baseball with his men at St. Nazaire.

A Journey in France

Arriving at the railroad station, we found our train ready. It was a little better than we had expected, being made up entirely of third class coaches, and as we got aboard we congratulated ourselves upon our good luck. Had the entire regiment been moving, we would have found box cars but, as it was only a battalion, the coaches were given us.

We started about 4 p.m. and the following morning we halted while the cooks made coffee for everyone by the side of the tracks. Although we had coaches there was no heat in them and the hot coffee, together with the corned beef and hardtack, did much toward warming us up and reviving our spirits.

Our train was not a fast one (in fact, not many French trains are) and, as we rode along, everyone enjoyed the scenery. We rode all day and did not stop for food, eating hardtack and corned beef when we would feel hungry.

The villages are very close together and from one village to the next, every bit of ground was found under cultivation.

There are no lonely farmhouses along the roads as in this country, and one rarely ever sees a fence. I have counted fifteen villages from the road upon which I was marching, and was not upon a hill at the time.

Life in the Villages

Everyone lives in the villages, and the houses are built in two parts; one part for the family and the other part for the stock. Each morning, someone of the household, usually the old grandfather or grandmother, takes the dog and drives the cattle out to the farm land to graze, returning in the evening.

These little villages have two or three small stores that sell groceries and, usually, about four times that number of cafes or "bavettes," where one can purchase light wines and beers, and, if one wants something stronger, cognac. Tobacco is very hard to get in France, and they only have a very poor grade, which is not cured and flavored as ours. Clothing and dry goods are brought from larger villages and cities by peddlers, who sell them from house to house. Some of the villages that we have passed through had not seen American troops before and, when they found that we were from America, they nearly went wild.

Final Camp Training

The following morning, we arrived at our destination, a large artillery training camp which is called "Camp de Coetquidan" *located in Brittany*. American artillerymen were sent there in large numbers for training in the use of the French cannon which were used by a great many of our soldiers. We were sent there to do guard duty over ammunition.

Before we hardly had time to remove our packs after arriving in camp, we were assembled and warned as to how we should regard the various things that were to be found around the camp.

We were told that we would find plenty of unexploded projectiles lying about and that we must never, under any circumstances, touch any of them as several lives had been lost by fellows who, like ourselves, had seen them lying around about and picked them up, explosions resulting.

All day long, we could hear nothing but the boom of cannon in practice and the whirr of aeroplane motors, as they flew about reporting shots and correcting the artillerymen in their work. It seemed to us, then, as if we were at as noisy a place as we could find. I found out differently

We were at this camp a very short time, as our regiment was put in the French army, and, after being assigned to a division, we were ordered to leave and rejoin the remainder of our regiment which also had orders to proceed to a point near Vitry la Francoise, which is very close to the front.

Moving Near the Front
March 12, 1918

In due time, we were on our way again and, after a ride of two days and two nights, we arrived one evening at Vitry. As we were getting close to the front, we did not proceed beyond this point until it began to get dark, as enemy "avions" (flyers) might sight the train and drop a few bombs on it. While we were at the station, railway officials came and told us that there must be no lights of any kind, as they would give away our location and cause the loss of many lives. As soon as it began to get dark, we pulled out and proceeded very cautiously toward our destination and, as we moved along, we would see trainloads of soldiers who, like ourselves, were going to some part of the front. Camouflaged cannon, mounted on railway cars, filled us with interest and here and there along the tracks we would see a grave which told the awful story and, as we went along, these graves began to get more and more frequent.

Everyone being tired, and not having a light by which to see to do the various things that help soldiers to pass away many a lonely hour, all hands fell asleep, and, when I opened my eyes in the morning, we were at a standstill in the freight yard of a medium sized village, which I later found was known as Givry en Argonne.

Warned Against Spies

As soon as possible, after everyone had detrained, we were lined up and given a few instructions regarding the country we were in and how we should act, so that, if we should run into a spy unexpectedly, we would know what to do, etc. We were told that it was only a short way behind the front line and that occasionally a German spy gets behind our lines and then, changing his uniform for that of a Frenchman, wanders about getting information about our troops, until he is satisfied and returns. Troops, who are going to the front for the first time, are apt to be talkative, and what appears to them to be nothing becomes valuable information when placed in the hands of the enemy.

Sleeping in Billets

March 15, 1918, 3rd Battalion took station at Remicourt

We had a hike of one kilometer (3/5 of a mile) to the town which was to be our home until we went forward. Up here, where the cannon roar night and day, we began to think the end of time was at hand.

Up until this time, we had always stayed in barracks but, up at the front, they are known as billets and are barns, houses, chicken houses, sheds and any place imaginable that will keep the rain from falling directly in the face when one tries to sleep, and I have seen many that did not ever do that. The advantage of quartering troops in these little villages near the front is easily seen. The enemy is constantly flying overhead and, if barracks were built, they would either be shelled or bombed the first time troops were put in. These villages, which are nearly all deserted by day; the enemy flying over gets no sign of life behind our lines, as the men are not allowed to wander about the streets.

In each village, there is a man who is known as the "Town Major," who has charge of the billets in said village. Each house or barn is numbered and capacity plainly marked upon it. If there are 500 soldiers coming to stay all night he marks down on a sheet of paper the numbers of the houses that these men are to occupy.

Before troops go to a village they send what is known as a billeting officer, who takes from one or two men from each company with him. He gets his list from the town major and then sub-divides it, giving each company representative his proper quota. These men, after locating the billets, go to the edge of town and await the arrival of the troops. As they come through the town, they are dropped off at their respective places without confusion. Occasionally, troops get into town in the middle of the night, soaking wet in a pouring rain, and find that there has been a misunderstanding as that the town is already full of soldiers. Then there is nothing else to do but march on to the first empty town. I have experienced this and can say that it is not a pleasing situation.

Such was then we were billeted in this village, which was at one time a beautiful place of perhaps 800 to 1,000 inhabitants but which had been reduced to less than 100.

Preparing for the Trenches

Two days after our arrival there, we were told we were to turn in all our American equipment and receive French *(March 14)*; also that Frenchmen, who had seen service at the front, were coming to give us special courses and prepare us for the trenches in thirty days. This did not seem possible, as the National Guard regiments were receiving six months training and, as we had been doing most everything except training, we knew practically nothing.

We began turning in our equipment at once, getting its equivalent in French at the same time. Everybody lost heart when they received the French rifle *(March 22, 1918)*. The American is a most accurate weapon and carefully made, it weighs 8.58 lbs., and is very expensive. The French rifle is cheaply made, is about 8 inches longer than ours and weighs much less. The bayonet has no cutting edge like ours and can only be used to pierce, while ours pierces and will cut right and left. *The regiment was issued three-round clip, Berthier rifles.*

We spent the first four or five days of our allotted thirty getting equipped. In the meantime, the men were classified in regards to the particular kind of training they would take up. For instance, a good ball player would be made a grenade thrower, a man with mechanical ability would be assigned to machine guns, automatic rifles, etc. Anyone who had operated a switchboard or similar work, would take up telephones; athletes would study liaison, and so each and every man was put at that particular work for which he was best fitted. When the instructors came, they found us waiting and anxious to learn so that we might get up where we heard the constant roaring of cannon and could see the heavens light up at night, as Fritz would send up a star shell light.

Instructed to Kill

The French instructors who came to our regiment were equally divided among the companies and at once began their work of teaching us how to kill without being killed.

The soldier as a rule is sometimes careless and indifferent to the drills he is forced to go through, but we, who were within hearing of the big guns that were belching out death and destruction daily, proof of which could be seen in the ambulances which came along filled with wounded, began to look upon it seriously and no one would feign sickness in order to miss a drill as each one realized that something might be taught that day which would be the means of saving his life. In addition to receiving the very latest methods in warfare from these instructors certain men were selected from each company to go to school for a 4 week's course in some special thing and in that way became a specialist in the particular branch which they studied. These men were selected according to their ability or experience which would help them to quicker learn the particular work they were to study, for example; a good ball player, especially a pitcher, would be sent to study grenades and grenade throwing. This man would, upon his return, be an expert grenadier and, besides knowing all about the use of various types of grenades, would be able to further instruct the regiment.

Grenade practice.

A mechanic would be sent to study machine guns as his mechanical knowledge would help him in quickly learning all about that particular weapon, as these men must become so expert that, should a gun "hang up" (bullet become stuck), he could quickly take it apart and assemble it in the darkest night and under highest excitement. Others were sent to study bayoneting, telephones, wireless, gas, liaison, signaling and the automatic rifle.

We would be up before daylight and, immediately after breakfast, would go out in the fields of the surrounding country and drill until night, stopping just long enough to eat a hasty dinner. There would never be more than fifty men in a group and these groups would be widely separated, as the enemy would occasionally fly overhead at a high altitude, but not so high that the observer could not have seen a large body of troops with the powerful glasses that are used on scout planes. To be seen would mean that we would be treated to a shower of bombs and the result usually being serious, officers soon learned to have their men lie down and remain perfectly motionless until the enemy had passed over.

Moving to the Front

After being in a village for a few days, we would move up to another village and, in that way, we became accustomed to the noise and the conditions at the front. As we left the little village near the railway station and went forward, we could not help but notice that each one had less old men, women and children, until finally we reached Maffrecourt, which is about seven miles from the front line.

There were eight or ten civilian families that would not give up their home, even for the Germans. They consisted of an old man and his wife in nearly every case. I saw one baby and a young woman of about twenty.

I will say here that, in the most advanced villages that are inhabited, the population in nearly every case consists of old people who, I imagine, think they have not long to live and are willing to die in the place where they have always lived and which they cannot bear to leave behind with the priceless accumulation of a life time, which, in most cases, has to be done when they become refugees.

House and barn, Maffrecourt, France, July 1917.

The children and babies cannot wear the gas mask, as it is too large, and their mothers take them back out of the Z. of A. (Zone of Advance), as it is called. Hundreds of babies have been killed in these villages by gas because of this, and, as everyone knows, innocent and helpless women and children are the Germans' most prized victims.

Regiment Reorganized

As we had been moving up, our regiment had been reorganized, so as to be able to act as an independent combat unit. We were in no division and consequently had to undergo some changes that most regiments do not. Our regiment consisted of a Sanitary Detachment, one Supply, one Headquarters, one Machine Gun and twelve line companies. The twelve companies were divided into three battalions of four companies each. In the American army, they have what is known as Machine Gun Battalions and one of these is attached to a regiment but, as we had no machine gun battalion, we had to organize so as to get the necessary machine gun crews, as each battalion of a regiment works independently when holding a sector.

Training with Hotchkiss Model 1914 machine guns.

Accordingly, one of the companies in each battalion was made up as a machine gun company. The regiment machine gun company was turned into "Sappers and Bombers," whose duty it is to dig dugouts, bury the dead, etc. The supply company was increased to three times its size, as there was to be much more work for them up at the front as they have to bring long wagon trains of supplies (food, ammunition, clothing, etc.) up each night, returning to their base before daylight for the needed rest before making the trip the following night.

In some sectors where observation is poor, owing to hills and woods, this work can be done in daylight.

While we were in Maffrecourt, we received our first Replacement troops to bring the companies up to proper strength after the reorganization *(these began arriving on April 12, 1918)*.

We were ordered to turn in our barracks bags, which contained all our clothing, and only retain one suit of underwear and one O.D. shirt. Many of the men had personal things, but as we were under the belief that we would get them again they were left in the bags. They were never returned.

Billets in Maffrecourt

Narrow-gauge railroad that led from Maffrecourt towards the front.

COMBAT
Ordered to the Trenches

March 19, 1918, the 3rd Battalion left Maffrecourt and relieved 2nd Battalion in trenches at Main de Massiges

One evening, the platoon sergeants were told to be ready at 7:00 the next morning to go to the front to reconnoiter the positions, as we were to enter the trenches the following day.

This is a task which is not as easy as it may seem. When troops go into the front line to relieve other troops, there are many things that must be learned so that the new troops may be able to defend the new position, if attacked a few minutes after taking charge.

These officers and non-commissioned officers must get the necessary information while on reconnaissance, so that they may be able to give it to their men when they arrive. Each man, who goes on this very important job, must carry pad, pencil, compass and field glasses.

Arriving at headquarters of the unit to be relieved, guides are given so that these men may reach their destination without delay or confusion. Several guides are required, as nearly all of them go separate ways. Most people are, I think under the impression that the trenches are long ditches running parallel to each other, filled with men standing side by side with their rifles lying on the "parapet," as the dirt which is heaped up in the front is called.

You find trenches running this way from one fighting post to another occasionally but, more often, you have to go back and get in another trench that leads up to the next fighting post, which may be within calling distance.

Imagine two large trees with their tops trimmed off squarely and laid down on the ground with the tips toward each other and with a space between them varying from grenade throwing distance to one half mile, and you have an idea of the great mass of network that was laid on the battlefields of Europe.

The ends of the branches terminate in what the French call "groupe de combat," meaning combat group. The entire affair is handled at the trunk and, as the troops go in the line they are separated and this continues until the members who go in the G.C. (Groupe de Combat) varies from twelve to twenty-five. These G.Cs. are surrounded by great masses of barbed wire and the space between the G.Cs. is also thickly strewn with it.

Entering the Champagne Front

We made our first entry into the trenches in the Champagne sector and, the morning following the reconnaissance, we started upon our trip which was about nine kilometers. The roads upon which we traveled were heavily camouflaged and there was no danger of being seen. Where there is an open country in view of the enemy, the troops must go at night so as to take the positions without the enemy knowing it. Should they know that new troops were occupying positions which they knew little about, they would attack them and such an attack would almost certainly end in defeat for us, unless the men had been there for several hours.

The sight of those men that day as they marched to the front is one that I shall never forget. All the equipment was new and clean, having lately been issued in exchange for our American equipment. We had heard wonderful tales about the trenches where we were to go. France lost more men in Champagne than in any other place, and, being a more or less open country, there is lots of activity of all branches. The trenches were being held by French troops with whom we received our initiation. They maintained their same number of sentinels and we simply went and stood post beside them watching everything they did and, when possible, asking them various questions. As no one could speak French then as well as they did later, we did very little talking and most of our information was gathered from the many things we saw them do.

Partial map of Champagne Front – Site of 369th's service
Butte de Mesnil, Massiges, Beausejour, Virginy.

Trench Equipment

As we came into the lines, we brought everything that a combat unit requires, and our train alone was a very interesting sight. Our motive power was the traditional army mule, which had settled down to the routine of war and which could not be induced to hurry no matter how much depended on his doing so.

Our train consisted of ration wagons, rolling kitchens, ammunition wagons, medical carts, machine gun carts and liaison carts. All this was in charge of an officer, who would ride from one end to the other giving orders.

After we arrived at the point where the train could go no farther, we found a narrow gauge railway and plenty of cars, upon which our supplies were loaded and pushed to the front.

Off for the Front

The road leading up to the front in the sector we were going in was heavily camouflaged and we did not have to wait until night as is usually the case.

After an early breakfast, the battalion was inspected. This is a very important thing and is always done before entering the trenches as it is very important that every man have everything while on tour in the trenches.

As we went forward that day, everyone was filled with thoughts of the good old U.S.A. and wondering if they would be privileged to return down that road after the tour of duty or if they would be brought down in an ambulance as they had seen so many French soldiers. They did not think so much about the possibilities of resting in one of the military cemeteries, of which there are hundreds, as they are right at the front where we had never been. These cemeteries are very numerous and when one goes by and sees the row of dug graves, ready to receive the victims of the next patrol, raid or attack it does not encourage him a great deal. They usually keep several dug ahead as they can never tell how many will be needed nor how soon.

We followed the highway to a point about two miles distant from the front line, then we left the road and entered the long winding trenches that would enable us to get almost within hearing distance of the Boche without being seen. The third line positions were also at this point and located on a hill. The side farthest from the enemy was nothing but dug-outs and all about soldiers were sunning themselves for, strange to say, it was not raining. The opposite side of this hill was nothing but barbed wire entanglements and, on the top, trenches were dug which, should the enemy break the other two lines in front, would be quickly manned by the men who were staying and as the Germans would try and break through the bar wire they would kill them with rifles, grenades, machine guns, etc., until they had enough of it. The men, who were there, were men who had been at the front and who were resting for ten days before going back again.

Reached the Second Line Trench

When we reached the second line positions it was quite late and we had to wait for our guides who were to guide us through the trenches until we came to the end of them and to the G.C. or stronghold.

The company is divided into platoons or sections, and sub-divided into half sections. It is one of these half sections that occupies a G.C. Our guides arriving, the half sections started off in the various directions.

One section remained at the second line or what is known as the reserve and also the field kitchen and Co. headquarters. I was Supply Sergeant at the time and remained with Co. headquarters.

Dug-outs were rooms built into the walls of the trench.

It was my first time in a dug-out, and became disgusted the first night. I had always imagined a dug-out as a large circular room with a fire built in the center of it which served to light as well as heat the room. Instead I found them to be tunnels with three tiers of bunks on either side and, although it is not always the case, I found that all the dug-outs were lighted by electricity.

There seemed to be a row of hills in this sector [Main de Massiges] and on each one there had been established a line of defense. The front line was on a hill facing a valley which was at the time "No Man's Land" and on the next hill facing us were the Germans. On the safe side of these hills were little dug-out cities and the second line had its own power house with power enough to light all the dug-outs. They would start the engine just before dark and stop it at 10 p.m.

My bunk was an upper one and I had no sooner gotten in it than I discovered that it leaked terribly owing to sweat [condensation], but I would not give in and so I slept until I got so cold and wet I could sleep no longer.

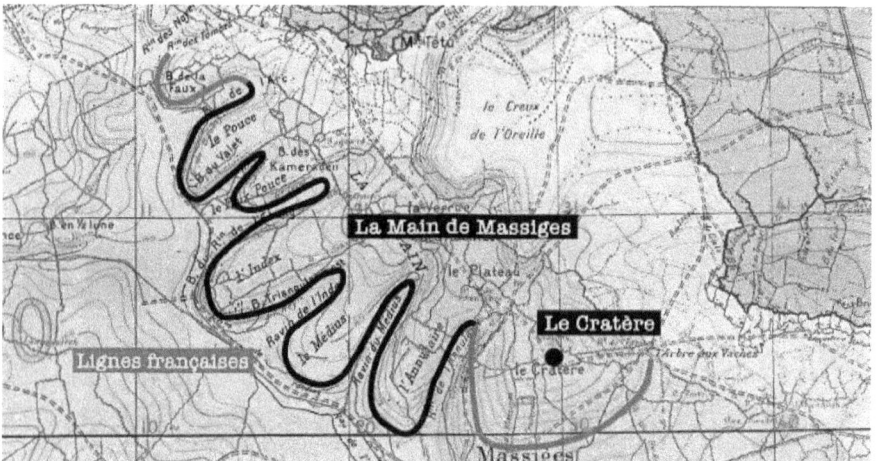

German lines at Main de Massiges, nicknamed the German Hand.

In the morning I went to the kitchen and while there saw the mess details as they came from the 1st line for breakfast.

It had been a quiet night and aside from a little machine gun fire and the star shell light of the Germans, everybody found things much better than expected and so it was quite a high spirited group of men who related their particular experience to the fellow in some other G.C. as they waited for the cooks to issue their rations.

Strongholds Well Supplied

In each of these G.Cs. there is ample ammunition to last several days should circumstances force them to lose communication with the P.C. (French abbreviation for the Post Commandant) which is company headquarters. There are all sorts of tools and equipment at these advanced positions to meet all needs, such as rubber boots for working parties when wet, pumps to pump water from the dug-outs, barbed wire to repair any that might be destroyed by shells, large metal boxes filled with emergency rations to be used when supplies are cut off in the rear. Those boxes are sealed and are not to be opened except by orders of an officer. When there is a heavy gas attack and Yperite *(Mustard)* or another of the most deadly gasses used all food becomes poison and when this happens it has to be buried and then sometimes the emergency food is eaten.

People wonder why one gets gassed after being trained to put on a mask in less than 10 seconds. If nothing but cloud gas were used I have no doubt but that everyone would be able to don the mask before getting gassed, but the Germans found out, before America entered the war, that cloud gas was costing too much considering the few who would get gassed during an attack that cost several thousand dollars, so they began sending it over in shells which upon bursting would liberate the deadly fumes.

Gas Attacks

All sentries on post in a G.C. are on alert for gas, and cloud gas is easily seen at a great distance, resembling a dense fog. It can only be released under favorable conditions, usually a wind blowing from their trenches toward ours at from 6 to 20 miles at best.

When the gas is released, it resembles a dense fog and as soon as it is seen the sentries begin giving the gas alarm by ringing bells, gongs or blowing large automobile horns that are fastened on posts for this purpose. As soon as these warnings are given everyone immediately dons his mask and does not take it off again until given orders by an officer who knows that the danger is over.

In the early days of the war the Germans would send men over who would, in the midst of an attack, tell them to take the masks off as the gas was over. The men could not tell and being anxious to breathe freely again would do so. A great many have been killed in this way.

The French soldiers who were holding the sector remained there and we simply put our men on the same posts with them to see what they did and to become accustomed to the new work.

One has a very strange feeling the first night as he stands at his post and sees the rockets go up that he knows are from the German lines.

Men standing at ease next to gas horn. Notice the French soldier with them. There was close comradeship among the men.

First Night in Front Lines

You speak to one another in whispers as a patrol might be near and if heard would learn your position. I remember the first night I spent in the front lines. I had been in the reserve position two nights and as it was very quiet I decided to see if I couldn't find a little more activity. Accordingly the following evening I saw the company commander (Capt. H. Fish, Jr.) and told him I wanted to go up to the front for the night. It happened that a sergeant who was up there was wanted in the rear to take part in an entertainment so I was sent up to relieve him, which I did. We had several men on posts at points quite distant from one another and it was my duty to go from one to the other all night and see that reliefs were made and that everything was alright. It was nearly dark as we went into position and we locked ourselves in the G.C. by closing gates which dropped in the trenches and fastened from the inside.

All night long the enemy kept sending up rockets which made No Man's Land as light as day, except for about two hours during which time they had a patrol out. They wanted it kept as dark as possible then so their men would not be seen. We could hear them as they would signal from time to time. This signaling is done by whistling to imitate some bird, and if a patrol separates, each park knows just what to do by the information given by pre-arranged signals.

Patrols

Patrols are sent out every night by every unit that is in the front line, and quite frequently two enemy patrols meet. When this happens a battle takes place in which no assistance comes to either side. Both sides know by the grenading, etc., that patrols have met but they dare not fire as the chances would be equal as to whether they would kill friend or foe and so, when they meet they must fight it out alone.

These patrols are sent out for the purpose of securing information and are exactly the same thing as scout duty in the days of the Civil War with the necessary changes that present conditions have forced them to make.

The number of men of a patrol differs, though from 6 to 10 is usually a fair-sized patrol. These men meet at a given point and there they are told what they are going to do. Each man carries a bag of grenades and an automatic pistol, but grenades are the weapons most used because they can be thrown in the midst of a group of men and no one knows anything about it until it explodes and then they can do nothing because they do not know from which direction it was thrown.

These men go across No Man's Land and lie around the Hun's G.C. and find out all they can. Sometimes they go behind them, passing very quietly between the two, and watch them at work for hours. They note conditions, and many things that would seem of little importance to a great many people are of the greatest importance there as they are sent to the Intelligence Department along with information gathered by other patrols at other points and the whole thing put together is in many cases an open book to those men of the Intelligence Department, who helped win the war with photographs, sketches, etc., just as much as the fellow who was at the front. If it had not been for these men we would not have known when the Germans were about to make their attacks and, not knowing, would not have been prepared. To have not been prepared would have meant annihilation but we always knew when an attack was coming and always prepared for it by strengthening the positions in the sectors where the attack was coming, being reinforced with additional troops, artillery, etc.

When one of these patrols goes out they have a place selected for their return and the troops at that point are informed at which hour the patrol will return. Some signal is agreed upon so that there can be no doubt as to their identity when they return which might be either earlier or later than anticipated, all depending upon whether everything develops according to plans. I can truthfully say that it doesn't always and many times a patrol comes in carrying and dragging dead and wounded comrades. Once discovered, a patrol has a very difficult task ahead as rockets are sent up one behind the other keeping it as light as day and a harassing machine gun fire is kept up, which forces you to crawl all the way back and it is no pleasant job to drag a dead or wounded comrade in this way. While you can drag a dead man without hurting him, you have to be careful with a fellow who may be mortally wounded, and usually you have a certain amount of respect for the body of one you had grown to like.

The identity of troops is concealed as much as possible and so dead men are never left unless absolutely necessary as the enemy would discover them the next day and go out the following night and get them in order to get as much information as possible from any papers, marks, etc. that might be on them. Occasionally it happens that a patrol is forced to leave a body and the next night both sides go for it. Great battles have resulted from such causes but will not go down in history. Although, to those engaged they presented as much excitement as any of the larger ones, they dwarf into insignificance when compared to some of the battles which lasted for several days.

Seeing the value that is put upon a dead body one need not wonder why men spend half of the night crawling two or three hundred yards with a corpse exposing themselves to enemy fire and a similar fate.

As one stands at his post in the blackness of night and hears that whistle which he knows comes from the lips of a German his nerves are all a-tingle and he strains his eyes to catch a glimpse of the patrol that he knows is there somewhere. You also send up rockets but it is only luck if you ever see anything as all patrolmen know enough to throw themselves flat and remain there until the last bit of light is gone before moving again. Should you happen to send one up at a particular time when they would be in an exposed place you might catch them but rarely never as exposed places are always avoided by them.

When morning comes you breathe a sigh of relief and as you are relieved by a few men who are needed during the day when everything is quiet, you go to the dug-out and get your drink of hot coffee, which the day guards went to the rear and brought up before going on duty, and smoking a cigarette you go to bed.

Observation Balloons Used Extensively

During the day, it is usually quiet, except for an occasional shell from the artillery where a battery happens to be well concealed. If it should be so situated that the smoke could be seen, they cannot fire during the day, as their position would be easily located by the aeroplanes that are always looking for these things, or the observation balloons that are up from daylight until dark, taking careful note of every sign of life that is shown behind the enemy lines, as far as their powerful glasses will permit.

These observation balloons or sausages, as they are called, because of their shape, are located about five miles behind the lines and from five to eight miles apart. One or two men go up in the basket and all day long they watch the enemy. When the artillery fires, they tell them what effect the shot had and in this way the range is corrected. They are held in place by cables and they telephone to the station underneath them all the information that they secure. Because of these sausages, all movement of supplies, ammunition, guns and troops have to be accomplished at night. The men who are engaged in this work are usually men who are no longer fit for active service in the front.

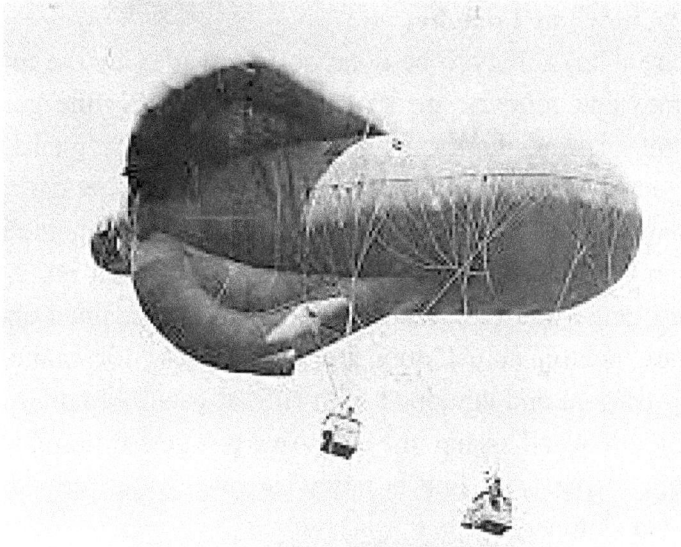

The French army had lost so heavily that they had to find ways of using some of the partially disabled men and this is one of the jobs that many of them do.

The men, who go up in the basket, have a parachute attached to them which is adjusted ready for instant use at all times, and very often a German plane will swoop down out of the clouds, set it afire and go back to its own lines. I have seen several of these big balloons set afire and, unless you happen to see the plane maneuvering around it and anticipate what is going to happen, it is gone before you can turn around. I do not think that the observers have any means of defense, relying upon the anti-aircraft guns to protect them, and when the Boche succeeds in getting over our lines that far; which is easily accomplished by flying so high that they can barely be seen and the motor not heard at all; he (the observer) is at the mercy of the German, and the instant he notices the balloon settling [descending], he has to jump as the gas in it is flammable and it is gone in less than a minute.

An observer is rarely ever caught napping, as he can hear the whirr of the motor before it reaches the balloon.

Sleep and "Chow" in Trenches

There are many things to be done during the day by the men in the front lines and relieves are so arranged that everyone gets an equal amount of time, both on and off duty. A few guards are maintained during the day and, as soon as it begins to get dark, this number is increased. But from midnight until daylight, the time during which most of the raids and surprises are carried on, a very heavy armed guard and the greatest vigilance is maintained and all men who are not on actual duty are in readiness for immediate action, fully dressed and equipped with rifle at hand. Although they may be lying down and asleep, the sleep that one gets from midnight until daylight in the front line is not what one would term as the most profound slumber.

KITCHEN AND DINING QUARTERS IN TRENCHES, MAY 4, 1918, BOIS D'HAUZY

About 10:30, those who have been sleeping more or less since midnight begin to stir about and soon everyone is up and ready for dinner, the first meal of the day which usually reaches the front about 11:30 or 12:00. There is no certainty about the food as the details occasionally get in direct line with one of the H.Es. (high explosives) of the Austrian artillery, which so ably assisted the Germans during the war. When this happens, another detail is sent out to investigate, and they bring the sad news that [the men] will be unable to get any food until the evening meal, as the dinner was all spilled on the ground and there is no more prepared at the kitchen. They might add that incidentally the men, who had been on the detail, were lying scattered about where they had been blown. The result is that we are S.O.L.* (Army slang, meaning, soldiers out o'luck). Everyone feels down hearted the remainder of the day, as it is generally known that a meal missed in the army can never be made up. *Peterson cleaned it up for publication; real meaning is shit-out-of-luck.

Making Dug-outs Habitable

After dinner, everybody gets busy cleaning up the dug-outs, trenches, etc. The ammunition expended during the night has to be replaced and camouflage has to be replaced and improved. In the early days, the trenches were the muddiest places imaginable, but before the close of the war, they were, almost everywhere, duck boarded, and travelling was made much easier. These boards are made by taking two 2x4s and nailing narrow strips across them. As the earth loosens from the sides of the trench and drops, it gets underneath these boards and prevents water from running, and these have to be taken up and cleaned out very often. When there is no other work more important, troops are always set at this.

All officers are instructed to better the conditions of these G.Cs. during their tour of duty, so that when they leave, they will be better than when they came. As troops are constantly changing sectors, they are constantly improving with the result that in some places, where there have been no drives and no advancing or retreating, one finds quite comfortable places.

I shall never forget my first night in a dug-out in a G.C. I was very tired and the fact that the water kept dripping down on my bed was enough to discourage anyone. The bunk itself was made of five wires stretched across and one of these was broken. I was very sleepy and would sleep a few minutes and the pain caused by the wires cutting into my side would wake me up. Turning over, I would try the other side until again waked up. I did this until I could stand it no longer, and so I got up and watched the rockets until day.

Most bunks are made of chicken wire and are fairly comfortable. The dug-outs are very damp and two or three days after a heavy rain, it begins to soak through the roof and then you are uncomfortable until it all soaks through. Since it rains nearly all the time over there, you are usually uncomfortable in this respect.

In the Champagne sector, the soil is almost pure chalk to a depth of from 18 inches to 2 feet in many places and the least little rain makes it very sticky. Sometimes one gets eight or ten pounds of this on his feet and, with eighty or ninety pounds on the back, one has little fear of being blown off his feet by anything less than an Austrian "88." [These were actually German '88's.]

Conduction of Raids

The third night we were in the trenches, the French regiment, with whom we were getting our final training before taking over a sector of our own, made a raid on the Germans and as all raids are, in general, the same I shall describe this one so that the reader may know the purpose of same, how it is conducted and what the result is – sometimes.

The purpose of a raid is to secure prisoners, who, when captured, are taken behind the lines and questioned by the Intelligence Department, and in this way an army is able to get news not only from the front but from miles behind the lines where patrols cannot reach and where the aeroplanes or the eye of the observer cannot go. Careful notice is taken of the general appearance of these prisoners and the changes from time to time are noted, and this way, a good idea of conditions can be ascertained. For instance, it was seen that the new steel helmets worn my men captured in the summer of 1918 were not as heavy as in 1917. Why weren't they? We could come to but one conclusion and that was that they were getting short of material.

It is quite an easy matter to send a party of men across No Man's Land with orders to kill one or two men who, patrols have found, are stationed at a particular point which they can exactly locate on a map. But it is a far different and more difficult task to get these men alive, as they will fight until they die in nearly every case unless so attacked that they have no chance to do so.

In this particular raid, they decided to use thirty men and the patrols had found out that a short distance from the main body of the G.C., there was a small post occupied by two men armed with rifles and grenades. It was connected to the main part of the G.C. by a trench and was well protected by barbed wire in front, the rear and sides.

The raiding party moved out from our lines around midnight and, with absolutely no noise, made their way to a point near the wire surrounding this position.

The artillery had dropped two or three shells in the wire at this point and made a sort of pathway through and expert wire cutters did the rest. To be an expert wire cutter, means to be able to cut this wire under the very nose of the enemy without making a sound, and anyone who has ever cut a piece of wire knows how difficult this is. These men have specially padded wire cutters and a man on either side holds the wire so that, when severed, it will not jump and, hitting other wires, attract the attention of the men in the post.

A raiding party gets at the designated point sufficiently early to enable it to do anything that may be needed preparatory to the raid, but not so early that they may be unnecessarily exposed should an illuminating rocket be sent up nearby. It is so planned that the men will be in a concealed place while waiting for the raid, but, if the terrain is of such a nature as to make this impossible, they must trust to luck, and the war Gods.

The artillery had been instructed as to the exact location of the post and the time they wished the barrage as well as the length of time it should last. The last is based upon the length of time it is estimated they will have made their get-away.

The watches of both parties are synchronized and as the moment approaches, the raiders get ready to spring into action at the bursting of the first shell.

They know, of course, that the smoke and noise of the bursting shells will be intense. Shells will be bursting all around the position except at the point where the party is to go in. It is impossible for these men to get away or for reinforcements to come up as so many guns are concentrated on this little spot that not an inch is left untouched.

Anyone who has been near a large stone quarry when they are putting off a series of blasts, can get some idea of the noise made by several batteries firing at the same target, by imagining something ten times greater than the quarry blasts.

The success of the raid depends upon the amount of surprise this terrific bombardment creates. Usually, before the men have time to collect their wits, they are prisoners.

An Unsuccessful Raid

This particular raid to which I am referring, worked out as planned up to the point when the barrage started. Immediately, and before the raiding party had time to approach and capture the two men, they began firing their rifles and one bullet striking a bag of hand grenades, which was carried by one of the men, exploded them, killing three instantly. The officer, who was in charge, was wounded by another bullet and soon everything became confusion. The two men on the post continued firing and that was sufficient to deter any attempt at capturing them alive and, in order to get away, they had to be killed, which was quickly done.

The raiding party lost no time in getting back with their dead and wounded. One of the men, who assisted in the killing of the Germans, brought back a helmet and rifle which he proudly exhibited the following day, as he boastfully told of how he killed their owner.

There are several reasons why this raiding party lost no time in getting back to their own lines, perhaps the most important being the following:

Should daylight find them still in No Man's Land, the Germans would easily kill them all. As soon as their barrage stopped, the men in the G.C. proper could rush out to this post and attack them. As soon as the Germans realize that a raid is being made upon them, they get word back to the artillery and immediately they place a barrage in front of the position that entirely encompasses the raiders.

Then, when our barrage dies down, they rush out and make a fight that can have but one result to the raiders, whose retreat has been cut off and who can seek no cover, but must stand without protection and fight the Hun who is in trenches or a well-fortified position.

These, I think, are the three paramount reasons why a raiding party must work quickly. A raid is a matter of surprise entirely and its success or failure depends upon the degree of surprise with which the raided are forced to meet the raiders.

Possibly this raid, the first one I ever knew anything about, with its poor ending, together with the sight of the victims as they went to the rear on their way to cemetery and hospital, left an impression that had a tendency to cause me to look upon raids as a part of the war game where the raider is taking all the chances.

While I have known of many raids that were successful, I have known of a great many more that were not. My regiment was in the front lines 191 days and, although raided several times, we came back without having a prisoner captured. Perhaps a prisoner is worth several lives. If he isn't, I think most prisoners captured by raids have been dearly bought. The day following the raid, we had three of our men taken to the rear seriously wounded by the explosion of some hand grenades in a dug-out. A Frenchman kicked them downstairs as he was coming down, while the men tried to get a little sleep after a hard night on post. *(Occurred in late April, see Capt. Fish's account in his May 1st letter to his father, Appendix Three.)*

Disposal of Wounded

During big battles, men sometimes lie wounded on the battle field for days without attention, and a great number of lives were lost that might have been saved had the "First Aid Packet" been applied at the time and thereby stopped the flow of blood, or kept out the infection which result in so many deaths from what were, at the time of the occurrence, simple wounds.

When holding a sector, things are done differently. The wounded receive immediate attention and many wounds that would result in certain death on the battle field are cured, because of their timely treatment.

In the foremost position, there are what is known as "First Aid Men." These men are members of the regiment, who received special instructions in giving first aid and who dress the wound as soon as received.

CHAPEL IN SECTOR HELD BY REGIMENT, MAY 4, 1918, BOIS D' HAUZY

Most casualties are during the night when holding sector, the result of raids or shrapnel wounds caused by artillery, which is also most active at night for reasons previously stated. Wounded men are placed in dug-outs, bandaged and made as comfortable as possible to await the coming of day and the trip back to the first aid station, where a doctor makes an examination and, if necessary redresses the wound.

The name, rank, number, regiment, company, etc., of the wounded, are taken and entered on records of the station. A cloth tag is wired to each man's coat which also bears the above data and he is then ready for the ambulance that shall take him to the field hospital, which is located as close to the front as is practicable with safety. Here he remains until ready to return to duty with is organization, if not too seriously wounded. Should he be, he is sent to one of the base hospitals, as soon as he is able to stand the trip.

A soldier, upon entering a base hospital, is transferred to a casual detachment, from which he goes to one of the replacement companies. These supply men to the units that have to get men to replace those wounded and killed. In this way, the soldier finds himself back at the front ready to start over again. He does not always return to his former regiment which is nearly always his desire.

The reason for this transferring is to keep regiments at fighting strength at all times. A regiment can only have so many members according to regulations and, if three-fourths of them were in the hospital, it would not be in very good shape to go into battle. Regiments are quite frequently reduced to that extent during an engagement and, by transferring, they can get men from Replacement Companies to bring them up to strength and in that way keep their duty strength the same as company strength.

On our fourth day in the trenches, we saw our first dead and wounded and naturally our morale lowered but the following day we were unexpectedly taken out and returned to our rest billets in Maffrecourt.

Transferred to Rest Billets

April 24, 1918

Everyone was tired out after the long hike from the front, and when, at last, we reached our rest billets at Maffrecourt and were assigned to them, all hands threw off their equipment, undressed and, in twenty minutes, the entire village was wrapped in slumber.

No one, except those who have been in similar circumstances, can realize how a person enjoys the first night's sleep after coming out of the lines. Up there, one can remove none of the clothing and always has to sleep with one eye open. When any unusual activity is noticed in any of the G.Cs. nearby, a "stand to" is ordered and everyone must get up and go to his post. In some sectors, where troops are uneasy, (which is noticed by frequent raids, daring ambush parties, etc.) these "stand-to's" are ordered every night at midnight and then all hands remain on their posts until daylight.

EN REPOS, MAFFRECOURT, MAY 5, 1918

There is nothing whatever to worry about the first night when returning from the front. The people, who stay in some of these villages, are in constant fear, and justly so, for aeroplanes bomb these villages nightly and occasionally the Germans send over some gas or a few High Explosives, but to those who have just come from a place as bad as "Dante's Inferno," at least, it looks and seems like heaven, and they undress and let every nerve and muscle relax and sleep, sleep.

Everyone is allowed to sleep the next day until nature says enough and, when they finally get up, the remainder of the day is devoted to the cleaning of equipment which is usually in pretty bad shape after the tour of duty. All broken, worn-out, or lost equipment is checked and ordered so that everyone will be fully equipped when the organization goes to the front again.

Toward night, an inspection is made by the officers, and woe be unto the man who has not cleaned his equipment. A certain amount of rivalry exists between the men and this keeps everyone within the limits.

Meeting the "Cootie"

We were located about 5 kilometers from a delousing plant, and, the following morning, we started to get rid of our newly found acquaintance, the "cootie." Who has not heard of the cootie? This animal is sometimes called "seam squirrel" by the American troops and, by the French, he is known as "to-to." The only difference between the cootie and an ordinary louse is that one has military training and the other hasn't.

He inhabits any place where soldiers have slept at the front, as well as the clothing of soldiers of every nation. He feeds on the blood of any soldier he can get on and has a wonderful appetite. As soon as troops get in line, they get lousy and, from that day, they look forward the time when they will be relieved and given an opportunity to get rid of them. The process is very simple. These delousing plants have ovens where clothing is put, then steam is turned on for thirty minutes, and at the end of this time, no cooties are left alive. While this is being done and the time needed to identify clothing, everyone takes a good shower bath, and, as he marches back to camp, he enjoys himself and hates to think of going back to get them all over again. But he does, and it is only a couple of days after going to the front that he is just as bad as ever.

Work While "at Rest"

While at the rest billet, the time is utilized for drilling and training the men in the finer points of warfare. As time passes, the method of defense against a certain offense that has been successfully used for a long time is of no use, as the enemy schemes a way to overcome said defense. Consequently new methods have to be employed, and it is while in the rest camp that they are taught to the men.

Perhaps the reader pictures a rest camp as a place where soldiers go to have a good time and to have their time occupied largely by eating and sleeping. Far from it. The work "rest," as used here, only applies to the nerves which are constantly on the alert when in line. While they are resting, the other parts of the body are kept busy. Every day, the troops drill and learn more and more about how to kill and how to avoid being killed.

Any activity, either offensive or defensive, that might have occurred while in line will be discussed in detail, all mistakes pointed out, and the correct procedure explained, so that the same one will not occur again.

In this way, the men gather many points, and each time they turn their faces toward the Hun, they are better fighters than before. All new regiments that go into the lines are sent to quiet sectors at first, and there they do little except defensive fighting. But, as they become seasoned, they gradually get on the offensive and soon they patrol, conduct raids and finally go over the top in real battle.

Instructed by Sham Battles

One night, while we were in rest after our first tour of duty, the order came for everyone to be up for an early breakfast as we were to have special maneuvers and were to watch an experienced French regiment go over the top at daybreak in the same formation, and under conditions as near like the actual thing as possible.

Accordingly, the following morning at daylight found us out on the drill ground to watch the battle and to do the same thing ourselves, as soon as we saw how it was done. Our battalion was placed on a side hill overlooking the would-be battle field, and, on top of the hill were the officers of the French regiment who were to tell our officers, who were also there, why every act of the maneuver was made. Aeroplanes flew overhead and signaled to the soldiers below by means of rockets and received replies by the same means.

These sham battles are very interesting and instructive and the machine gun nests are very easy to capture, being nothing but flags stuck in the ground in concealed places and offering no resistance. They are much different from the ones they represent. Drilling kept up until one night when we were told to prepare for the trenches, as we were to go in the next day. So once more, we packed our equipment and again we turned our faces east. This time, we entered the Argonne forest near the edge of a place called "Bois de Hauzy."

Battle Practice. Note mix of French & American gear. French straps and ammo pouches, American canteens and even a web belt.

INTO THE ARGONNE

On Duty in the Argonne

1ˢᵗ Battalion arrived April 14, 1918 and was relieved by the 3ʳᵈ Battalion on May 1, 1918.

We had spent five days in the trenches and were under the impression that we had learned all there was to know about it, but, as soon as we entered the wooded section, we saw everything was different. In Champagne, the troops were hidden from the enemy by deep trenches, but in the Argonne, the trees formed a natural camouflage, which concealed all signs of life and activity.

Ferme de Monplaisir   Combat du 25 septembre 1915 en Champagne.   Bois d'Hauzy.

Wartime painting of Bois d'Hauzy, by François Flameng.

In the Champagne, the G.Cs. (combat group) were deep trenches and, when attacked, one would throw grenades on to the ground above and around his position, for it many cases, the average man would not be able to see the earth from the trench, unless he stood on the firing step. In the forest, one found things about the

81

G.C. much different. Instead of trenches, they had breastworks made up of various things, such as ammunition boxes filled with earth and piled one above the other to required heights. Occasionally, you would find breastworks on the side of paths which were exposed to the enemy.

We relieved a regiment of French infantry at this place, and, by dark, they had all left and gone on their way either to rest or to another part of the front, and we found ourselves feeling very much alone, as it was to be our first night in the trenches without French soldiers, and, if attacked, we wondered if our inexperienced men would be able to withstand it or if we all would be slaughtered. Daylight finally came, however, and from each G.C. came the message, "Nothing to report."

Fortified line in Bois d'Hauzy.

Daily Reports Made

Reports are sent in from each combat unit each morning at daylight to Company headquarters. There they are consolidated and sent to the next higher unit. They are consolidated and forwarded in this manner until they reach General headquarters. There are several methods employed to get these messages to their destination, chief among them being runners, liaison dogs, pigeons, telephone and wireless. These reports cover the activity of the Infantry, Artillery and Aeroplanes of both sides, work accomplished, ammunition expended and losses suffered, and are submitted every twenty-four hours.

Kitchens Cause New Problem

One thing which caused the officers a great deal of worry in this sector was the problem of the kitchens. They were heavily camouflaged by the trees, but the trees also made good fuel, and the closer they stood to the kitchen, the better suited they suited the "K.P.," and he would not stop to think of the great danger he was exposing himself to by cutting them. The result was that avions flying overhead would notice a small clearing in the forest and that clearing would become a target for some of the long range guns as soon as he conveyed the information to the artillery. They became more careful after the Germans succeeded in landing one shell directly in a pot of chow and wounded three cooks, Needless to say, a new rolling kitchen was ordered at once and three more men were promoted to the grade of cook to replace those wounded in action. When the artillery gets ready to fire on one of these positions, an aeroplane circles over and, as each shot is fired, it signals the artillery by means of rockets until they can put them exactly on the spot. In this way, they find the range on various objectives and when the shadows of night camouflage the battery positions, they hammer away until nothing is left.

Getting the Elusive Aeroplane

The anti-aircraft guns keep the aeroplanes from flying at low altitude, but occasionally one gets pretty bold and flies low enough to take a photo which shows soldiers quite distinctly. These anti-aircraft guns are placed in concealed positions in every imaginable place, but especially on the hill tops, and are usually of about three-inch caliber. These guns throw shell which are filled with shrapnel and explode by time fuse. They throw the shells just ahead of the aeroplane and can fire in the neighborhood of fifty shots before a plane can get out of range.

I saw thousands of shots fired, but never saw one hit its mark. It is a difficult target and, besides estimating its speed, one has to guess its altitude and gauge the projectile so it will explode at the proper distance. A great number have been brought down by this type of gun, however. They have a tendency to make aeroplanes fly high and thus prevent them from getting too clear a photo. It was not a rare thing up at the front to see a long patch composed of puffs of smoke graduating from the first shot fired, which has been in the air sometimes and is very large, to a very small puff from the last shot fired, and just in front of this last puff, it you look closely, you are apt to see a plane travelling "full speed ahead." As it goes, puffs of smoke keep appearing just behind it, denoting that the anti-aircraft is still on his tail.

Occasionally a plane gets low enough to be in range of a machine gun. The only chance they have of hitting him is to set it so as to fire in a space through which he will pass. Aiming at the airman would be worse than useless.

First Days in Trenches Lucky

We were very fortunate while in the Argonne, losing comparatively few men in the three months that we held a sector there, much to the amusement of the French, who could not understand it. On our right there was a regiment of troops from Morocco led by French officers. These men may not make ideal soldiers, but they are excellent fighters and absolutely fearless.

On our left, there was a regiment of Alpine chasseurs or "blue devils," as they are called. France looks upon her blue devils with the same respect that Germany does her Prussian Guard, or the United States her marines, and the fact that both of these regiments were being raided frequently, suffering heavy losses, while we between the two went unharmed, was more than the French could see into .

The 369th served with French regulars, Chasseurs,
Moroccans & Senegalese.

It was while in this sector that two of our men defeated and put to flight a German raiding party of twenty-four (according to the newspapers) in a hand to hand encounter with bolo knives and hand grenades as the main weapons. This incident proves to what degree of danger men will go when on a raid (previously described) to secure a prisoner.

Colored Troops Excite Hun Curiosity

No one cares to believe two men can whip such an overwhelming number under circumstances at all normal, and they couldn't.

This is the explanation: We had not been in the trenches long before the Germans knew that a strange organization was opposing them, but they did not know who we were or from whence we had come. They had seen and learned to fear the black soldier who came from the colonies of Africa and who delighted in cutting off ears, fingers and noses from their prisoners and tying them around their necks. But here was a regiment of black soldiers wearing the United States uniform, English gas mask, French helmet and equipment and who spoke English. There was only one way. That was to get a prisoner and let him solve the mystery. This I think, explains why these men did not kill the two men when they offered resistance, hoping that they might be able to capture them without killing. They were of no use to then dead and, in trying to capture them, they suffered so heavily they were forced to withdraw before reinforcements came and killed all of them.

Peterson here is describing the well-known heroics of Sergeant Henry Johnson and Private Neadom Roberts during the very early morning hours of May 15, 1918 while manning a listening post in No Man's Land.

Senegalese soldier with a bolo knife,
of the type used by Sgt. Henry Johnson.

Period map of this sector, 1914. French entrenchments along northern border of woods. The line at the right, near the bridge, was likely where Johnson & Roberts were located on the night of May 14-15 when the enemy attacked their listening post.

The Monotony of Holding Sector

We remained in this sector until the last of June, quietly holding sector, and each week it became more and more monotonous. Now and then a raid with its large or small toll of dead, depending upon how successful it was, occurred. Occasionally, a man or two would get killed by a shell and a few sent to the hospital with gas, but really nothing happened to break the monotony of trench life. One would become thoroughly disgusted when he sat and thought it over. Sitting and lying around with the enemy within calling distance was enough to discourage anyone. The war could have gone on forever this way, and the French seemed quite contented. While they got a permission which gave them a week home every four months, we had to be content with letters which arrived at irregular intervals and sometimes not at all, dated sometimes six weeks prior to the date of receipt, during which time the writer could have died of old age or almost anything else.

The latter part of June, it became generally known that the Germans were planning the biggest drive of the war and, about July 1st, we were taken out of the trenches, being relieved by French troops and were told that we were going to another part of the front to help hold the Germans back. We all felt that the monotony was broken. *The 3rd Battalion marched to Courtemont on July 1, 1918, just over a two-mile march on a straight line.*

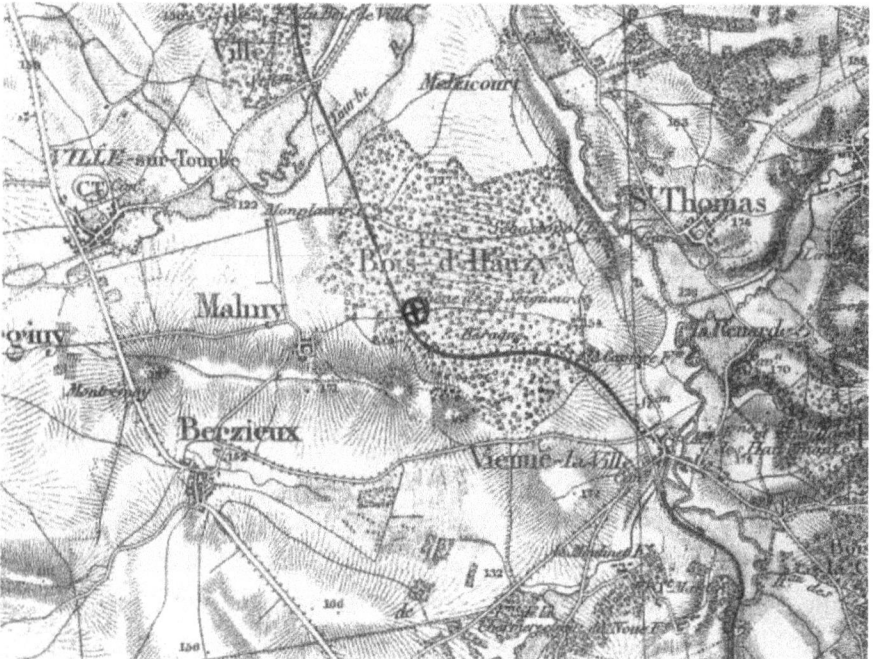

Wartime map of Bois d'Hauzy and
nearby villages where the men were stationed.
Regimental HQ was in Vienne-la-Ville.

Evacuating Towns in War Zone

After being relieved by a regiment of French soldiers, we returned to our rest billets at Maffrecourt again.

Here we found that everything indicated that an attack was expected. The few families that had been living here all through the war were at last forced to leave by orders of the French government, who made all civilians vacate the villages that were in the zone they figured would be heavily shelled by the enemy.

It was a pitiful sight indeed to see these poor people with their horses harnessed to their largest wagon loading on as much as they could of their earthly possessions. As the wagons would get to the point where they could not hold much more, they would look at first one piece of furniture and then another, undecided which they would take. I remember one old man and his wife (the last to leave the village), with whom I had become quite well acquainted, whom I watched as they loaded their wagon. They had, upon all previous occasions that I had seen them, seemed to be rather contented with everything as it came, but to me it looked as if the leaving of their home was taking all the joy out of life for them. After they had loaded as much of their furniture and small farming implements as they could, they tied two boxes to the rear of their wagon which contained their winter supply of meat in the form of tame rabbits which a large majority of the people raise over there. After they had given them an abundant supply of grass they got on the wagon and started on their journey, which would end when they came to a place where they could find suitable shelter.

As we watched then going down the road, we wondered if they would ever have the privilege of coming back to their home again, and, as they turned around for a last look at the home they were forced to leave, it filled everyone with a determination to do everything in his power to preserve those homes, so that someday they could come back and enjoy their old age, that which they had toiled for in youth.

SECOND BATTLE OF THE MARNE, JULY 1918

Preparing for the Drive

Things were rather quiet for the next few days, as is always the case just before a big drive, when it seems as if both sides are resting and saving ammunition for the big event. During these few days, our side kept brining up guns, both big and small. It seemed to us as if all the artillery in the world was being concentrated on this particular sector. We were taken from Maffrecourt to a small village known as Courtemont. Here we found they were doing the same thing. All night, artillery would pass on the way to the front. These guns were taken into the fields and camouflaged, so that, when daylight came, the German aviator could see nothing.

Each cannon has quite a large force of workers to keep it in operation and besides the men, there are several horses (at least six) that are used to move it from place to place and to keep it supplied with ammunition after being placed. These horses are kept in the rear out danger and each night they bring up ammunition with them and take a load of empty shells back. This is very hazardous work for the drivers, who must make this trip each night, as the Germans shell all the roads at about the time they think these ammunition trains are on them.

Heavy field artillery.

Although this extra artillery that was placed to reinforce the regular batteries did no firing, they were getting their loads every night and one can imagine that those which were placed two weeks ahead had an abundant supply. In addition to the horses, motor trucks were also running all night bringing their loads of death and destruction.

Although we knew that the Germans were concentrating all their best divisions along this sector to make this drive a success, we felt pretty safe after seeing all the artillery that would begin firing on No Man's Land the instant they began stepping over their parapet.

It would be quite a difficult matter for me to picture the way this mass of artillery looked and to describe the feeling of security it gave us men of the infantry who had to go up in the front and stop those, who lived to pass the heavy barrage, with bullet and bayonet.

These guns were placed according to caliber; in lines parallel to the front, with very little interval between them; beginning with the 75s which were within 3 miles of the front to the mammoth naval guns, mounted on railroad cars, which fired shells weighing 1400 pounds and were several miles back.

Plans Made to Fool the Hun

From the best information the intelligence was able to get, the drive was supposed to be launched early in July, but the first ten days passed without any signs of activity, except the usual patrols and raids.

My regiment was billeted perhaps six kilometers from the front and each night, as it began to get dusk, we would sling our equipment and march about three kilometers to positions from which we were to make the supreme sacrifice trying to defeat the Huns. The positions at the front, which were quite a distance from ours, were occupied by French soldiers during the day and until 12:00 o'clock at night. Then they would retire to other positions on a line with us, leaving us as the foremost troops, and the first the enemy would meet when they came over. This plan of defense was worked out by Marshall Foch, because, if the front line positions were held, everyone would be killed during the artillery preparation as there were no dug-outs at the front, except those on top of the ground, which resembled somewhat of the old-fashioned dirt cellar.

When the drive started, the Germans would rush over and by the time the newly established line would be reached the men would be fatigued, consequently, they could not fight so well. Besides, all the artillery preparation would be wasted on positions that were not occupied and from which everything of value had been taken. This was the reason these positions were held until midnight. Perhaps you wonder why they held them at all. It was done so that the enemy would not know of the method by which they were to be defeated. Their patrols would have soon discovered that the front was not occupied and then they would have penetrated our lines until they came to the occupied positions. Of course, the Germans would not have been foolish enough to waste hundreds of thousands of dollars in ammunition on empty trenches.

Awaiting the Attack

As days passed and no attack was made, the French began to wonder what was the matter. About this time, information was collected from prisoners captured at various points to the effect that it would be made on "Bastille Day," which is a holiday occurring on the fourteenth of July. Each night we kept going up to our positions, reaching there between 8:00 and 10:00 p.m. and remaining until daylight, when all danger of attack was over. We would then return to Courtemont and spend the day in sleep. In these positions which we went to each night, there was a large quantity of emergency rations to be used in case we were forced to remain there for several days. Everyone carried a canteen of water but the weather was so extremely hot that there would be little left by the time we reached the position. On the 12th or 13th of July, the Intelligence department gave out the information that the attack would start the morning of the 15th. The artillery preparation, which they said would be very heavy, would start on the evening of the 14h at 11:53 p.m.

The 14th being a holiday, the French Government issued champagne to all her soldiers, and my regiment, being with the French, received it to the extent of one bottle for every four men. This had a tendency to cheer the boys so that everyone seemed in the best of spirits and apparently were eager for the fray in order to know what the fates held in store for them.

The Drive Begins

That night we started for usual for our positions, but were ordered to move back. We returned to our billets and went to bed to enjoy a good night's rest. At exactly seven minutes to twelve, we were awakened by what seemed to us an earthquake but, upon getting awake, we found the cause was shells exploding.

In a very short space of time, the orders came for us to get up and fall in with full equipment and proceed to the front as the drive had started.

Second-line trenches at Beausejour (Berzieux). These secondary trenches were manned by a support battalion of the regiment. One battalion at the front, one in support and one at Maffrecourt for rest & repose.

In a few minutes we were on our way and everyone experienced that strange feeling that comes to every man before you go into battle. We had gone about half the distance when we came to the edge of a large field through which we had to pass. This field was filled with cannon and the Germans were evidently trying to put them out of business before they started over the top. As we came to the edge of this field, we could see the flashes of light as shells burst here and there. We were marching four abreast and were at once ordered to spread out, as a shell dropping on the midst of a large group would kill many. We began going to the right and left and the cry of "Gas" went out. Everyone immediately put on his gas mask and in the darkness of the night and the dense smoke we became lost and separated. But as all knew the way, everyone reached his destination in a short time, except a few who were killed and wounded.

The company was divided into four parts and stationed separately. As soon as company headquarters were established, the company commander began sending out liaisons to see if the various units reached their destinations. It was at this place that I decided I would never become a liaison, unless forced to become one. Their work is usually easy but, when travelling, is most dangerous and they travel most of all.

We were forced to send out three before any returned. The shelling was intense, the air was full of smoke and gas, to say nothing of the darkness which made travelling difficult enough. One of the runners reached the first post of the three he was to visit and fell at the door of the dug-out overcome by gas. He was taken inside and delivered his message before becoming unconscious.

As we sat in the dug-out waiting for the first streak of dawn and the first wave of German infantry, everyone examined rifles and bayonets and filled cartridge belts with ammunition from the supply kept in the dug-out, while the shells were whistling and bursting outside.

The men felt better than the officers, because they did not know certain things which the officers did. The enlisted men knew that we were about three kilometers from the front and were under the impression that there were French regiments in front of us. Believing this, as they did, they felt quite safe, as they knew that the Germans would have difficulty in reaching us in great force. In reality, we were the first line of defense as all the troops in front had withdrawn at midnight. The officers knew that it would be nothing short of a miracle if any of us were left to tell the tale, as troops have lots of spirit at the first part of an attack, being usually half crazed by drink, and they come forward with such momentum that they go through several lines of resistance before they are stopped. To be taken prisoner was not thought of in Marshal Foch's plans, and we were expected to fight until killed.

We had just one chance. Along with other information gathered by the intelligence department, was that the miles of front along which the Germans expected to drive. We were told that they figured the infantry would come no further than about two kilometers on our left. This was not to be depended upon, however, and, although we knew that the artillery would extend a considerable distance beyond this to protect their flank, we thought that the bombardment would be lighter than at the point of attack. This bombardment was not at all light and we felt that there was little hope in this respect. At last, it began to get a little light and we listened to hear the machine guns and rifles which would indicate that they were coming. It kept getting lighter and lighter and yet no Germans appeared.

The boys began stepping outdoors to look around, not venturing far from the door as shells were still falling all about. German aeroplanes came over in large numbers to see the result of their bombardment and to note our activity.

We knew then, that we would see no infantry, as it was daylight, and the machine gun and rifle firing which we could hear on our left told us plainer than words that they had come over at that point and that, as we stood and listened, men were giving their lives to make the world safe for democracy. I shall never forget the sounds of those guns that morning, as I stood and tried to picture in my mind the terrible scenes which were so close to me.

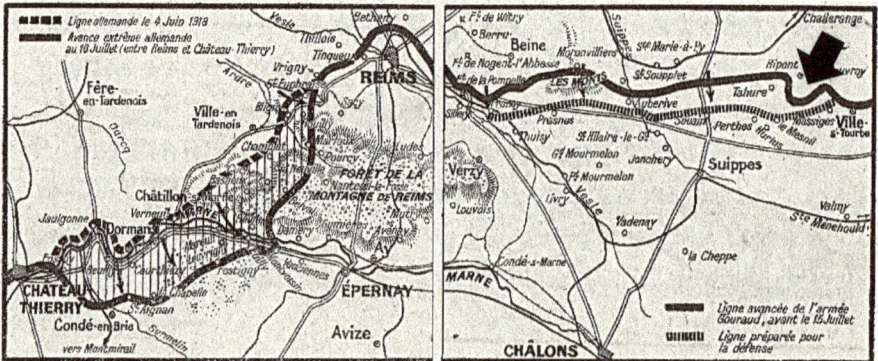

German offensive of July 15, 1918. The 369th was stationed just south of Ripont. The German bulge at that location was due to General Gouraud's defense-in-depth. To the west was the German advance to Chateau-Thierry, where the US Marines earned immortal fame.

The Tragedy and Humor of War

About 6:00, the bombardment began to slack a little and a runner came from a section of our company which was stationed on our left to report that they were alright and that the runner who had been gassed during the night was being brought in. He was on stretchers and in bad shape, foaming at the mouth, eyes closed and breathing like one who had just finished a marathon. We also had at our post a man who had been slightly gassed and wounded with shrapnel in the leg.

It was decided to get them to a little village about a quarter of a mile away where there was a doctor. Four men carried the stretchers and another fellow put the wounded man on his back, and at about the same time they started, the artillery began to increase again. They had gone about one-quarter of the distance when shells began falling a short distance in front of them so fast that they could not

96

advance. They would start to the right and a shell would land in front. Then they would turn to the left, only to be forced to turn again by another one. Everyone was in the dug-out except Captain Fish and myself who were watching their progress. We were up near the top of a hill and could tell about where the shells were going to land by the sound of their whistling. Finally one came along which was very low. The stretcher bearers evidently thought it was coming near them for they stopped. A burst of smoke enveloped them and, when it blew away, all that could be seen was a mangled mass of what had but a moment before been men. A few minutes later, one moved and finally got up and hobbled back to us. He was wounded in many places but none of them were serious. *(One of the stretcher bearers killed was 22-year-old Ludlow Luther, a draftee replacement from Ohio; he had joined the regiment in late April. His body was returned to the US in 1921. Another was Marshall Scott of Virginia – he received a posthumous Croix de Guerre for his bravery.)*

There was nothing for him to tell. The shell, he said, struck about three feet in front of them and, when he came to, the other four were dead.

All this time, the many who had been carrying the gassed and wounded fellow had been zigzagging back and forth trying to get forward when suddenly a shell burst about sixty feet from him. The fellow, who was on his back and who had not been able to walk at all, got off his back and the last I saw of him, he was leading the first aid man in one of the fastest foot races I ever saw.

We remained in this place until afternoon, when orders came for us to go back to Courtemont. We got there and were ordered to go to a place called Hans. Arriving there, everyone threw himself down and slept. We were about five kilometers behind the lines and to the left of Courtemont. Directly in front of us was the place where we had heard the machine guns and rifle fire in the morning when the attack started. About 11:00, we were awakened and ordered to fall in with full equipment. We were going forward and to the place I had tried to picture in my mind earlier in the day. Little did I think then, that I was going to see it so soon.

March to the Front

I shall never forget the march to the front that night. We had been under the most trying nerve strain for the last twenty-four hours, being under shell fire almost constantly. To march up to the front that night on a road that was being kept hot by shrapnel from the enemy was not a pleasant thing to think of, much less to do, and I feel sure I speak for everyone when I say we were not at all anxious to do it but orders have to be obeyed and under the darkness of night we went forward. A real sportsman enjoys entering into a game when he can match his wits against that of the adversary, but travelling on a road swept by shells of guns miles away offers little chance for brain work. There is no chance to fight back. All one can do is proceed and if anyone gets wounded or killed, let the Medical Department care for him.

The three battalions of my regiment had been placed, during the drive, one behind the other, in what are known as first line, support line and reserve line and as we had been on first line for several days it was our turn to go in as reserve.

To equalize the strain on all, these units kept rotating, being in each position for ten days. It was now our turn to go in reserve, which we did and we were behind the other two battalions of the regiment. After marching about two or two and one-half hours we were halted along the road and it seemed hours before the Frenchmen, who were in the dug-outs nearby, vacated them, so we could get in.

In reality it was only a few minutes but shells were bursting in the air above and shrapnel was falling all about. Occasionally one would "clink" as it struck a steel helmet and bounced off.

The men were exhausted and were satisfied to lie anywhere under cover. I well remember the dug-out, I was in; [it] was made of elephant iron, as it is called, and was about twenty-five feet long. The men were so packed that no one could say that someone was not lying on some part of him. My legs furnished head rest for two fellows but no one protested and soon everyone was asleep. A large number of dug-outs are made of this iron, as it is easy to construct a fairly safe shelter in a short time. It is made of heavy corrugated iron and bent so as to form half a circle about twelve feet in diameter. These are bolted together and then covered with earth.

The kitchen crew brought food to us in the morning but everyone preferred sleeping to eating and so the food was left untouched. In the afternoon another supply of food came up from the kitchen and as everyone had awakened it was eagerly devoured. Soon after eating, preparations were made for moving as our battalion was to go into the reserve position of the regiment.

The kitchens were located about three-fourths of a mile to the rear and as the officers did not know whether there were suitable places for kitchens where they were going it was decided to leave details to locate kitchens, get food and then find the battalion.

As the battalion moved forward that night I was told to remain behind and was given twelve men with orders to find the kitchen and bring food to them on the morrow, provided I could find them.

Third Battalion field kitchen December 1918, Ungersheim.

Bringing Up Food

The next morning we went to the kitchen and getting several cans of coffee and a good supply of bread we started to find the battalion. The men of my detail were all new men, who had recently come to us as replacements, and were under fire for the first time *(April replacement companies from Texas. Louisiana, Virginia, Missouri, etc. were joining the unit at this time)*. It matters little how brave a man may be, until he has become accustomed to having shells burst about him, he is apt to do considerable dodging until he gets used to it. I shall never forget my first trip with food. When a shell would whistle, no matter how far away it might be they would drop their burdens and throw themselves in the gutter. It would take quite a lot of talking to get them out again and when they would get out they would fairly fly until another shell would cause them to take cover. We carried food in this way for several days until the kitchens were moved forward.

The battalion was located in and near a small town called Minaucourt *(arrived there July 21. 1918)*, which was sheltered from shell fire, somewhat, by hills. We would carry the food to this village and under a shed which afforded shelter from shrapnel we would distribute the food. This shed was also used as a morgue and each morning we would get there with breakfast as they were bringing in the dead or shortly after.

The first ten days after we arrived in this sector there was not a single morning that the morgue had less than five dead in it and one morning sixteen. These bodies would be buried the following night, consequently new faces kept it from getting tiresome, as we used to examine these dead Germans (sometimes Frenchmen or men of our own regiment) very carefully to see if they had anything of interest to us on them and to see where they had been hit.

The second or third day we began to get some news from the first line and support positions from the boys who came back for supplies. When the drive had started the enemy had come over and finding our artillery too heavy, had been forced to halt after coming two or three kilometers. They found plenty of good dug-outs that had been abandoned by the French and they took possession of them. These dug-outs had been mined and several hours after the drive started and at a time when the French knew they would be well occupied they were exploded and the artillery was trained on them. When our men went into these positions, they found dug-outs and trenches filled with dead soldiers, who had been caught in Marshall Foch's trap.

Dead Boche.

As is the case immediately after all attacks, there is plenty of activity. Raids and counter-attacks are nightly occurrences and our men found this to be equally true with this one. The enemy had gained lots of valuable information during the few hours they had been in possession of our lines, and snipers had found out the various portions of our trenches that were exposed. As a result we lost several men in certain sections of trenches as they were passing from one point to another. German aeroplanes would fly close to the earth over our trenches, defying the machine guns, and would pour their deadly volley into our men at the rate of 500 shots per minute. In this way, we lost some men.

Many German Souvenirs

Any of the boys we chanced to see would have plenty of German souvenirs, which they had taken from the dead up where they were, where, they said, the Germans were heaped in some of the dug-outs and in others had been buried alive. I had some rather exciting times with my food detail as they would become frightened and spill whatever they might be carrying and on several occasions the men at the front had to be content with half rations. I remember one place along our route in a swamp, there was a shell hole filled with water and all around the hole laid the rifles, helmets and equipment of three French soldiers. It was not necessary for anyone to tell us what had happened there and it mattered not whether there was any shelling going on or not; when the men of my detail passed this spot they always quickened their step as if they were afraid this might become the scene of a second tragedy.

At the end of ten days we went into support and then days later into the first line, which, though not as lively as it had been, was still lively enough. Every night or two the Germans would come over and try to take a G.C. with all its occupants. Our kitchen was located a little over a half mile from us which we reached by a winding trench about eight feet deep.

Relieving the Units & Sgt. William Butler

As the roads were shelled so heavy at night that the supply trains did not always get through, one of my jobs was to go to the kitchen each night and find out if they came [through] O.K.

It was while I was on one of these trips that the boldest raid I ever heard of was attempted by the Germans and defeated by the courageous fighting of one man. We had been in this sector for several weeks when orders came to Regimental Headquarters, one day, that we would be relieved by French troops that night. As the enemy had been getting information about reliefs in some mysterious way every time they were made, the greatest secrecy was maintained in regards to this one as the Germans would shell the communicating trenches so that losses would be suffered by the relieving party coming in and the relieving party going out. None of the enlisted personnel knew of this except the very few "all wise," ones who were connected with the various units' headquarters. The lieutenants and sergeants in charge of combat groups were notified as to the approximate time at which they might expect to be relieved.

Later in the evening *(August 18th)* and not long before the time planned, word came that the relief would not take place. This word was not conveyed to all the small units in the foremost positions as no one could leave until they were relieved.

I had gone to the kitchen after finding that we were to remain, to see if supplies came all right. I stayed there until about 1:00 a.m. and as that was long past the time for when them to come, I decided not to wait for them and so started back to P.C. I had gotten about two-thirds of the way back when I heard a noise, which, upon listening, proved to be someone approaching at top speed. Before I had time to decide what to do he came around the corner and I saw that he wore an American helmet. Perhaps by this time he was the more scared of the two and as he slowed up I asked him where he was going. He didn't tell me but said that I had better not go up there as the Germans had come over and wiped out one company. After giving me this advice and information, he rushed on, leaving me as much in the dark as if he had said nothing.

I had heard no artillery and only a few machine gun reports and could not believe that there was much fighting without some noise so I went on. When I got to our P.C., I found everyone up and ready for action. This surprised me still more and upon inquiry I found that the Germans had raided a G.C. and that part of my company had gone in to reinforce them. It seemed that the Germans had found out, in some way, which will always remain a mystery, that we were to be relieved. They had come over and got behind a G.C. and into the trench leading up to it, and deliberately walked in saying that they were French soldiers to relieve.

Another party in the meantime had captured the lieutenant and five men. The sergeant *(Butler)* to whom the German lieutenant spoke, did not, for an instant, recognize the difference in uniform. A soon as he did however, he succeeded in reaching an automatic rifle and killed the Lieutenant and four men. Then he assisted in recapturing the men who the Germans were staring back with.

The following night we were relieved and from the terrible amount of shelling along the roads and trenches, it was evident that the enemy knew it. I was left to look after the kitchen and supplies and when we finally got loaded we found that a good sized van would have had no spare room. As it was we had everything piled in and on the rolling kitchen. The next thing was to get someone to ride on the kitchen to see that the things did not fall off. No one cared to do this as it made so much noise (being all metal) rolling over the macadam road, that it would be impossible to hear a shell. I took my place on the little step on the rear which is provided for that purpose and we were off. The drive was a little anxious to get out of the danger and he soon had the horses running. We lost five cases of bacon but he would not stop to pick it up and I, being anxious to get out also, did not urge him.

Under ordinary circumstances each company has a supply wagon on which to carry these things but we could not use ours as we were short of horses, having had a shell fall in our stables which was five miles behind the lines and kill three men, thirty-six horses, wound six so badly that they had to be shot and slightly wounded several others. We kept moving until daylight when we came to a village and billeted. We had remained for a couple of days and then started to a camp at St. Ouen, which is near Vitry-la-Francois. We were about a week making the trip. The weather was very warm and with our equipment which was quite heavy from twelve to fifteen miles a day was enough for all.

This was about the first of September and was the first time we had been out of hearing of the guns along the front since February.

While in position at this time, the 369th held a sector stretching 1,000 meters, or just over six-tenths of a mile.

German 88 millimeter cannon,
precursor to the famed "88s of WW II.

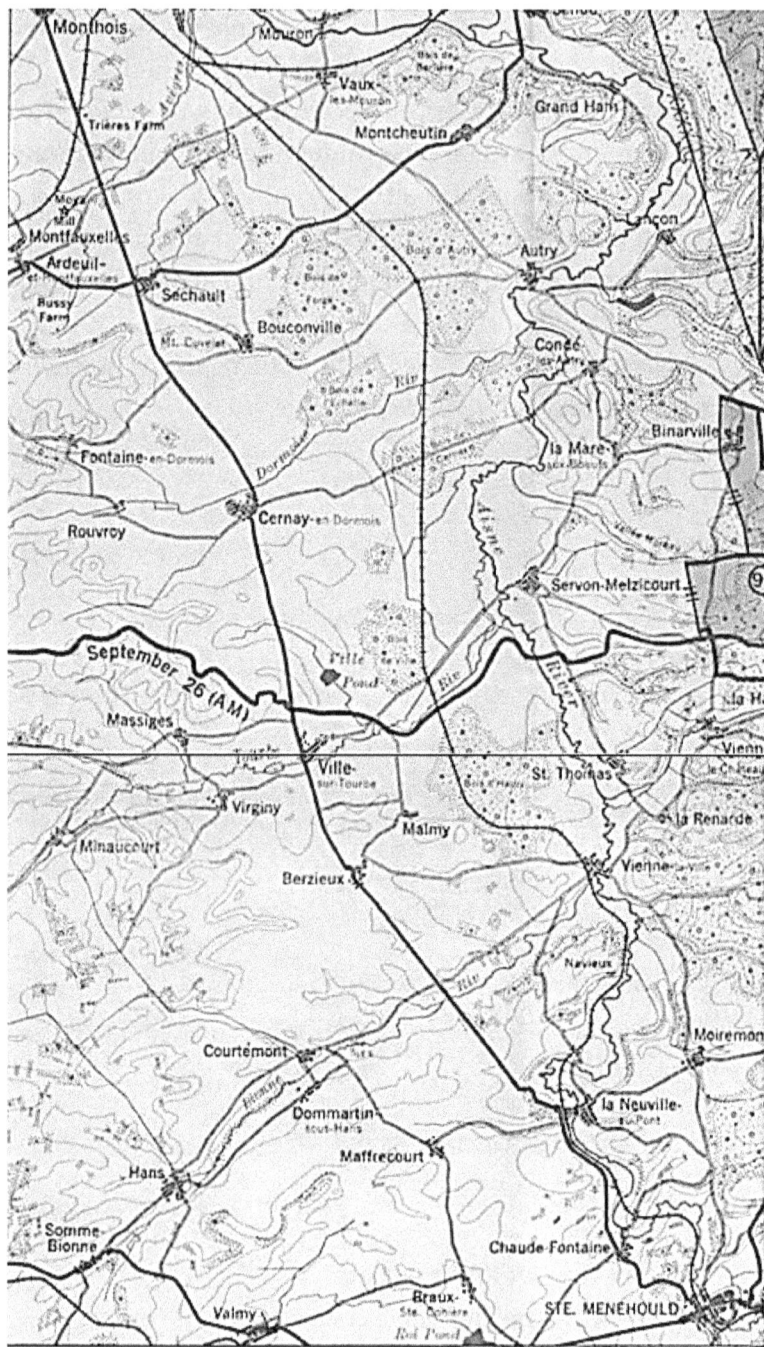

Operational area of the 369th during most of its service at the front.
The front line as of September 26, 1918 is shown.

To Join French Army

We had been in this camp but a day or two, when it was rumored that we were to become a part of the French army. We had up until this time only been attached to it but while we were in this camp we were permanently assigned to the 161st Division of the Fourth French Army.

All visions of American equipment, food, etc. vanished with the news. On our way to the from the front we had been told that we would probably go back into the American army and everyone was delighted with the thoughts of once more getting the real fighting equipment and food that tastes natural. The French army rations are substantial but very, very plain and not to be compared with that of Uncle Sam's.

As soon as we had been assigned to this Division we were ordered to move and we at once left and started back for the front having spent ten days in the quietest place we had been in for months.

Troops are always carried up toward the front and after one day's march we were carried to within a few miles of the place we had left but a few days before. The reason troops are carried up is so that they will not become discouraged by long tiring hikes and have no spirit when they go into battle and we knew that we were soon to go into battle as we had been told that our division was waiting for us to join them for that purpose. I shall never forget the all-night ride. There were perhaps one hundred twenty-five trucks and their noise, together with that of the pouring rain, drowned any other noise. We reached our destination about 2:30 a.m. and unloaded just outside a little village. No one knew in the darkness where we were but everyone was feeling fine after such a beautiful ride. As the trucks drove on and the noise of their motors died away we could hear the rumbling of cannon at the front and we realized that once more we were back. It all seemed like a dream from which we wished we had not been awakened.

The following day *(about Sept. 14th)* we marched up to Camp les Maigneux, where we had been so many times before and at once began training for open warfare, for we were to go into real battle, worse, perhaps, than that of any previous war.

Military transport trucks.

Training for an Attack

While we were training in Camp les Maigneux for the attack, we were treated much the same as all shock troops are prior to entering battle. *(Camp les Maigneux was two miles southwest of Valmy.)*

We were given new clothing throughout and nearly everyone was given a pass to one of the cities or large towns nearest the front. The training was not hard nor were the hours long. Sometimes we would start out in the morning and go cross country four or five miles in exactly the same formation as we would in actual battle with aeroplanes flying overhead signaling to us so that we would become familiar with them. We would signal in return and as we were not at it long enough for the novelty to wear off no one ever became tired of it. The food was unusually good and plentiful and with all this unusually good treatment everyone was in the best of spirits.

This was the way they wanted us to be and is the condition they strive to put all troops in just before going over the top as disheartened men are half beaten before they start. Everything possible was done to make the men feel confident of the success of the attack.

Daily bulletins were sent to all organizations at or near the front, telling of all important operations. These rarely ever reach a bulletin board, but while we were at Camp Maigneux all encouraging bits of information were read to the men daily and I feel certain that every enlisted man in camp felt sure that we would be successful. In fact we were led to believe that this would be the last big drive of the war and we all had visions of being home by Christmas. While it came very near being true in our case it was not because we had been told so or because we believed it as every regiment that has ever gone in battle has been led to believe as we did.

Americans Have Success

The Americans had just been very successful in gaining a lot of ground near Metz and a man from each company of our regiment was taken there and shown the well-fortified positions that the Huns had been driven from, and to hear about how it was done by the boys who had helped do it.

This particular drive had been very successful and although the Germans lost many in killed, wounded and captured, the Americans lost less than a hundred killed. The men who went from our regiment were picked privates, so chosen because it would be easier for the men to believe the than officers or N.C.Os.

The fellow who went from my company had many tales to tell when he came back; how the Germans were discouraged and ready to surrender at the first opportunity. He had some of their rations that had been left behind when they retreated, and everything he said had a tendency to make our men more anxious to get at them and finish the job.

Marching to the Front

Sunday night, Sept. 22, 1918, at ten o'clock, with a large per cent of the regiment comfortably sleeping, while the rain was pouring down outside, we received orders to pack and prepare to move out at once, and at 10:45 we were going toward the front under heavy marching orders. I have seen a great deal of rain in France; spent seven weeks in Brest and it rained almost every day. Army statistics claim that out of the 365 days of 1918 it rained 342 in Brest, but I feel safe to say that it rained harder this night than I had ever seen before or since.

We marched about 6 kilometers and bivouacked in a field just outside Somme Bionne, a small hamlet where our Divisional Field Hospital (French) was located, and about four hours march from the front lines. It was not a pleasant prospect that confronted us as we marched into the field and, being halted, were told to make ourselves comfortable for the night.

Under ordinary circumstances, every man would have had a half shelter tent which, when joined to another half made a fairly good shelter for two men; but we had received no ordnance property for seven months from the U.S. Government, being equipped with French equipment, and many of these shelter tents had been lost or destroyed during several months' active service at the front, so now we found ourselves forced to spend a night out in the open with no means of protection except the wet earth, and our equally wet blankets.

There was nothing to do but make ourselves as comfortable as we could. This we did, some lying down and other walking about till morning. Everything was so wet that it was ten o'clock before the cooks were able to give us some lukewarm water which bore the name of coffee.

There being no definite information as to when we would leave, we began making preparations for the night, and, with the help of the sun, which came out about three o'clock, we dried out some and erected various kinds of shelter, and spent Monday night a little better, though not pleasantly by any means. We received orders on Tuesday morning to heap our packs up in the field with our names written plainly on them, together with the various things that we did not want to take into battle. They assured us that they would be returned to us afterwards. Many of the men put their watches, etc., into them, rather than take them and risk losing them. No one ever received his pack again and almost everyone left his toilet articles, and no one expected to be able to have time to use them. When the battle was over, the men were marched by a heap (all that was left) of packs, about 100 kilometers from where we had left them, and after we had received several hundred replacements, and each man was ordered to take a pack. When my company arrived, all the packs were gone.

The Meuse-Argonne Offensive of the American First Army (including the old 69th NY, now a part of the Rainbow Division) and the French Fourth Army was directed to disrupt the main German line of supply. Cutting of this supply line would make the German positions west and northwest of Sedan untenable. Defending this line of communication was of utmost importance to the Germans, and their defense would be counted as some of the most brutal fighting of the war.

—✠·✝·✞—

BUTLER, WILLIAM O., Marshall, Fauquier County, Virginia.
Sergeant. Company I, 369th Infantry, 93rd Division.
Distinguished Service Cross; Maison de Champagne, 18th August, 1918.
Citation: "For extraordinary heroism in action near Maison de Champagne, France, 18th August, 1918. Sergeant Butler broke up a German party which had succeeded in entering our trenches and capturing some of our men. With an automatic rifle he killed four of the raiding party and captured or put to flight the remainder of the invaders."
French Croix de Guerre with Palm.
Citation: Similar to the American for the same deed.
References: G. O. 37, 1919; G. O. 51, 1919; War Dept. Records.

MEUSE-ARGONNE OFFENSIVE

Preparations for Launching Drive.

We received that afternoon such us we had not received before while in France. As we were lounging around, a Ford car drove in the field and two ladies got out and, opening the back of the car, began serving cocoa and cigarettes to the crowd that had already assembled. Soon everyone was in line and the two girls had no difficulty in getting rid of their stock.

Wednesday, we were issued our iron (emergency) rations and everything that we had lacked in the way of firearms, ammunition, signals, etc. There seemed to be an abundant supply of everything and everyone had five gas masks. It was evident that the drive was not far off, as all caution had been thrown aside and artillery, ammunition, field hospitals, etc., were not only being moved up all night long, but all day as well, although enemy planes were constantly flying overhead, finding out all they could.

That night we moved up toward the front and entered tunnels that ran between the first and second lines, and we were not permitted to step out in the open the following day at all. We had left our kitchens behind and were now dependent upon our Iron rations, which we ate that day. These rations consisted of fourteen hard tack, one cube compressed coffee, two cans corned beef, one cake chocolate, one cup sugar and one can solidified alcohol for making coffee.

As it began to get dark Wednesday evening, we began making preparations for moving up to the front line and then we knew that the attack would start the next morning. We had already experienced considerable suffering since leaving Camp les Maigneux, Sunday night and were much lower in spirit than when we had left there. Realizing, however, that we would not get any rest until the battle was over, the orders to go forward were gladly received by all, and, as we went forward, not a single sound was made, as we did not want the enemy to know that there was any circulation of troops in our lines. They knew, of course, that we were going to make a drive. Neither side made a drive during the war that the other didn't know about, but they did not know exactly when we were going to make it, and, even though it could not be a complete surprise, the greater the degree the greater the success.

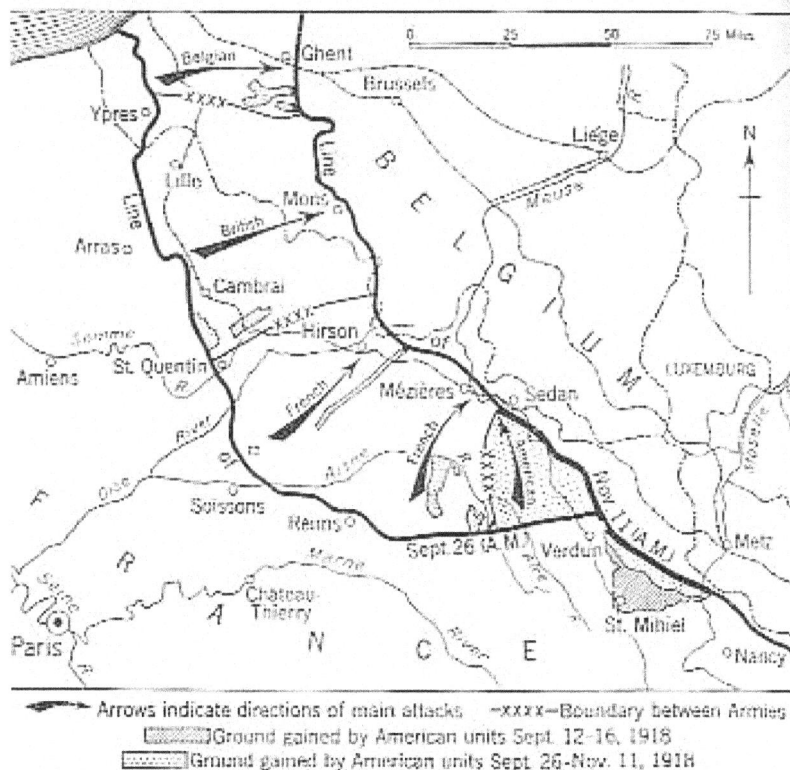

American and Allied Attacks on the Western Front
September 26–November 11, 1918

Arrows indicate directions of main attacks –xxxx–Boundary between Armies
Ground gained by American units Sept. 12–16, 1918
Ground gained by American units Sept 26–Nov. 11, 1918

The Meuse-Argonne Offensive. The 369th served with the French IVth Army, shown just west of the XXXX line bordering the Argonne Forest.

The Drive Begins

We had just reached our position, where we were to wait until the zero hour, which was but a few rods behind the foremost positions and were at the time held by a battalion of French troops of our division, when our artillery preparation, which was said to be the heaviest that had ever been given any troops, started. These shells were falling just in front of the first line and not many rods from where we were, and the bombardment began just as we had halted. It seemed as if every gun along the front fired with the first one and the men, not knowing it was our own artillery, rushed into the dug-outs pell-mell. Even down in the earth twenty-five feet, this terrible noise penetrated until one had to shout to make himself heard. All night long this steady fire was maintained along a front of ninety kilometers, and, as we sat waiting for morning, we felt that there would be little for us to do as it did not seem possible that life could exist under such fire.

I will not attempt to describe the feelings and thoughts a soldier has as he sits waiting for the fray, except to say that sinner and Christian alike believe that their fate rests with the Almighty One, and that no man goes over the top without having offered up some kind of a prayer. It was quite noticeable, while we were waiting in the dug-outs for moving, that there was no swearing or gambling going on, as there usually is when a bunch of soldiers get together in a dug-out with nothing to do.

About 2:30, the boys made a little coffee and ate some hard tack and began to get ready, as no one knew the zero hour. This is kept secret as long as possible, so that the enemy cannot find out. If they should, they would, at the time, place a barrage on No Man's Land so heavy we could not get through. This is one reason why the first waves of an attack are best, as there is little artillery to bother them.

As it began to get daylight, we began arranging the men in the proper points so as to be ready. We (my battalion) were the second wave, following at 800 meters the French battalion that had been

114

holding the position, and we were followed at the same distance by the other two battalions of my regiment, while behind them came the other battalions (French) of the division.

The formation employed for attacks in the latter part of this war was much different than that used fifty years ago. The deadly machine gun has made it impossible to advance in mass formation or even in the extended order as taught by our government in 1917.

Companies are divided in two parts, one forward and the other following at a distance of several meters. Each part contains eight squads of eight men each. (This is in accordance with French tables of organization, which we were under; American companies are larger and consequently have a larger number of squads.) Those squads are placed one man behind the other and one hundred feet between squads. To the enemy it appears as if there is one man by being so placed, and those men are taught to always keep behind the leader. Should he turn to right or left, they do likewise at the same time, and thus afford a very small target at all times.

The Zero Hour

As we were arranging the men, stretcher-bearers began coming back with wounded Frenchmen and we knew that the drive had started. At about the same time, a liaison came up from Regimental Headquarters to give us the zero hour. The note said that we should start at 5:25. The captain looked at his watch and saw that it was just 5:26. The noise was so terrific that the human voice was of no use, so, making the sign "forward," we were off.

Formation of the Battling Troops

As we started forward that morning, my company consisted of five officers and one hundred and ninety-six men. This is much less than an American company, which has six officers and two hundred and fifty-four men, but, as we were in the French army, we had to conform to their tables of organization.

We were deployed (extended, spread out) according to the French system, which, after trying many ways, they found to be the one in which troops could advance with least losses. The companies were divided into two lines, one three hundred meters in advance of the other, and each squad (eight or nine men) marched in single file lead by the corporal, with an interval of one hundred feet between squads.

At this stage of the war, attacking troops
were more spread out to avoid machine gun fire.

The officer, who commands the company, marches in the center of this formation and has what is known as "company headquarters group," which consists of runners, signalers, stretcher-bearers, etc., with him. These runners keep going from one section (platoon) to another, carrying messages.

The other two battalions were behind us eight hundred meters apart, and behind them came the Engineers and Pioneers to reconstruct roads, bury dead, salvage clothing and equipment, etc.

First Advance Made Safely

We knew that after we had gone a few hundred meters we were to halt one hour and forty minutes and everyone felt that he could make the distance to the first halt. Our barrage had lifted and everything was quiet, except for an occasional shell from the enemy, but we could hear the rapid and steady fire of machine guns some distance in front of us where the first wave was meeting feeble resistance. The atmosphere was nothing but smoke and gas and one could not see more than a quarter of a mile away. In the low spots, this was so bad that we had to don our masks before entering them, and this made it very much harder for us to advance.

We travelled at a very slow walk, and we had gone but a few yards when a shell landed near a squad, wounding three men, and this lowered the morale of all. We reached the "dead space" where we were to halt and, being out of the gas, everyone took off his mask and breathed a sigh of relief and a prayer of thanks for having finished the first lap of our trip safely. By "dead space" is meant that part of the terrain that is safely sheltered from enemy fire by reason of hills, etc., and it is always selected for stopping places, when possible, as troops are safe when in them.

As we sat there, waiting for the time to start again, we saw strings of German prisoners marching to the rear. In one of these groups there were about 225, who were guarded by two Frenchmen, one in front and one in the rear. Often times, they were sent back without any guards at all, as they abandoned all arms at the time of surrendering and were too glad to be out of the fight to make any trouble.

Watching these men go by brought back all spirit that may have left us when the three boys were wounded, and everyone became uneasy to be up and after them.

We advanced a distance of about five kilometers without mishaps and had begun to think that we would never catch up to the Germans in order to fight when, as we reached the top of a hill, we saw shells falling everywhere in the valley below and could hear the machine guns of the Germans on the hill across the valley, which was less than a mile away.

RIPONT—CERNAY-EN-DORMOIS AREA
Looking down Dormoise Valley, east from Ripont

Death Encountered in the Valley

In the center of this valley, there was a small stream which was known as Ripont *(Dormois)* River and along its bank grew shrubbery to a height of about eight feet. Aside from this shrubbery, there was no cover between the two hills, and to advance in the face of shot and shells under such exposed conditions at 10:00 a. m., with a hot sun to help fatigue one, was no pleasant prospect. However, we went on and got to the edge of the river when the terrific fire caused us to halt. We had no sooner reached this point than Major Spencer *(Third Battalion commander)* was grievously wounded by bullets, and simultaneously firing increased, forcing everybody to lay low. It soon became evident to us, that the Germans, who were up on the hill, had seen us as we advanced and had let us get to the river where they knew we had to cross by one of two bridges, both of which were kept under the most incessant fire.

As we lay hidden behind the brush, the bullets kept getting closer and closer and now and then someone would cry out that he had been hit, and with the shells that were bursting all around, it was plain to all that unless we get out of there and up against the steep bank of the hill in front of us, we would all be killed. Going back was out of the question. It was either cross one of the two bridges, and dash across a very bad swamp about three hundred yards wide, or lie where we were and be killed.

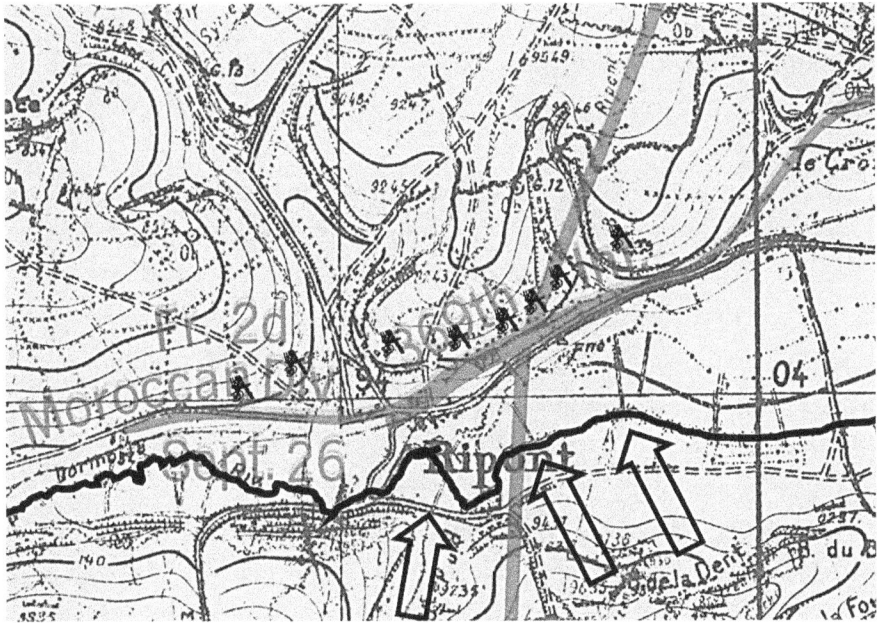

Crossing the Dormois River, arrow at left represents
Third Battalion's crossing at one of the bridges.
Rows of barb wire are also depicted as xxxxxxxxx.

The Dash for Life

The men began going forward by ones and twos, rushing across the bridge and throwing themselves in shell holes and the tall grass of the swamp as they began to draw fire by their activity. After lying a few minutes the firing would ease up and they would make another short dash. As we lay in the field we could see the French battalion, who were ahead, resting on the side of the hill smoking and talking. They had very few casualties in crossing this place, which at that time seemed impossible for us to do; because they were closely following the creeping barrage which kept the Germans under cover and reached the dead space before they could get out to use their deadly weapons.

I had been lying near battalion headquarters group, but after the Major, Adjutant and a runner had been wounded and another runner killed all within twenty feet of me, I decided that I had better locate in a safer place. I was quite heavily weighed down and made up my mind that I would dispose of some of it, as I had seen several fall trying to get forward because the weight prevented them from running fast.

I had been taught the value of everything that a soldier carries, and was at a loss to know which I could best part with, but finally decided to leave three of my five gas masks which I did after selecting the two best ones; and my blankets, which were really the greatest burden. These blankets, I reasoned with myself, I would not need if killed and if I kept them, they would be the cause of mv death anyway. I was quite willing to sleep a few nights without covering if by so doing, I could prolong my life.

After abandoning this equipment, I crawled near the bridge and remained quiet. I could hear the bullets as they whistled by and I noticed that at times there would be intervals of a few seconds during which no bullets would come near the bridge, I got this exactly timed and during one of these periods I made a rush. I had no sooner hit the bridge than the bullets followed suit and, as there was nothing for me to do but keep going, I did so, throwing myself in a shell hole as soon as I got across. I kept advancing by short rushes when it was quietest until I reached a place of safety.

Casualties Many on First Day

This swamp was strewn with dead and wounded men of my battalion and of the French battalion that had preceded us. When I finally reached the dead space that evening, it was eight o'clock.

I shall never forget a lieutenant who had been wounded by a machine gun bullet that morning and who had been carried to a place of safety where the wound was dressed and he was made comfortable. During the aerial activity in the afternoon, a German plane swooped down and began firing at us. Although there were perhaps fifty of us, only one bullet found a mark and that instantly killed the lieutenant, who was bearing up so bravely.

After it got dark, all who had not done so came forward to the dead space, and, when they had all reached there, I got the remainder of the company together and took the name of every man. When I finished, I found that I had 70 names, just 120 less than that morning at 5:45 o'clock.

The one hundred and twenty lay in the valley below, either dead or wounded, and those who were left worked untiringly until the last wounded man was carried out. It would be pretty hard to describe the feelings of these men as they went back and forth carrying them out, and, in the darkness, would occasionally step upon the dead body of someone hidden by the darkness and tall grass, or, upon going to a spot where they had left a wounded friend, would find that he had later died.

The Germans and Frenchmen kept putting up illuminating rockets all night to guard against counter-attacks and surprises. When one of these would go up, making the swamp and river as light as day, all working parties would throw themselves flat on the ground and remain there until it went out.

Although I do not know the exact casualties of the other companies of the battalion for that day, I do know that they were little better off, and that not less than four hundred men fell that day.

German machine gun nests held up the 369th from crossing the Dormois River to the capture of Bellevue Ridge.

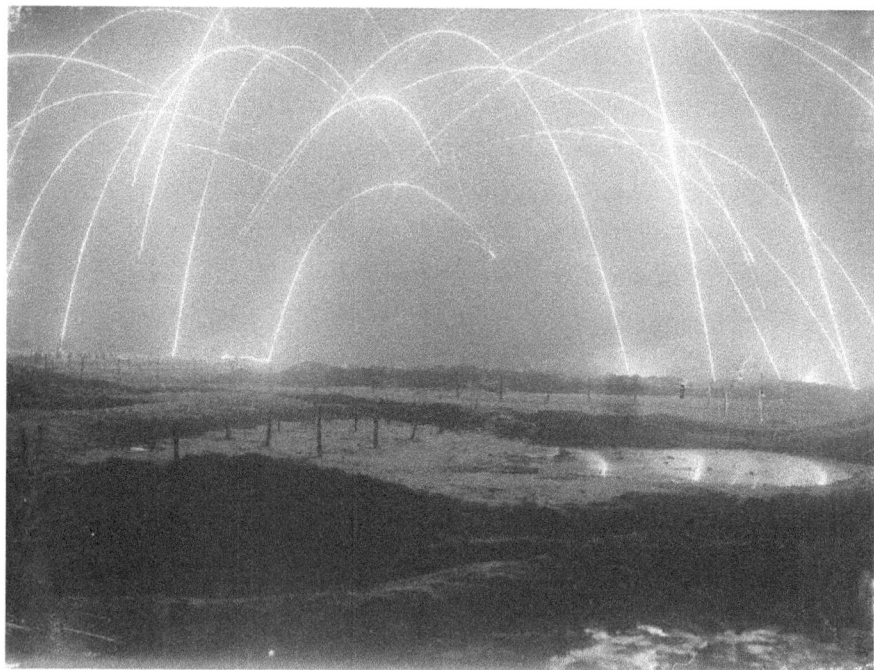

Illuminating flares; photo by British officer.

Solemnity of Facing Eternity

It was easy to see that, if this continued, we would all be wiped out in a few days and that night, as we lay down under the hill thinking of our dead comrades lying close by, we were changed men; far different from what we were that morning as we started over the top. Days like this add years to one's age and cause one to look upon life in a more serious light. Men, who had never thought of praying before prayed that night, and why shouldn't they?

We all knew that, with the first gray streak of dawn in the morning, would come that command, "Forward" again, and who knew but that was the last night they would ever spend on earth.

Methods of Locating Troops

The next morning we were held up quite late as we had advanced ahead of the outfits on our right and left and had to wait until they caught up with us. These orders came from divisional headquarters, where the location of each unit is known at all times, except in very rare cases like the "Lost Battalion." There are several ways of getting information as to the location of troops, even in the thickest lighting. As troops advance, telephones are kept right up on the firing line and operators take all sorts of risks to maintain connections. Homing pigeons are carried and released with messages in a small tin can strapped on the leg. Dogs are also used for this purpose, but, when all these fail, they still have the aeroplane which flies over and signals by means of rockets for troops to give their location.

About fifty per cent of the men carry panels of jalon, which is a piece of white oil cloth about ten inches by twenty inches fastened on two sticks, rolled up and carried in a little ease when not in use. At the signal from the aeroplane, these are exposed and present a white line along the ground when seen from the aeroplane, from which it is photographed.

This is done each night, after the advancing for the day is over and during the night these negatives are developed and printed and then the orders are issued for the various parts of the line to wait until other parts of it have advanced on a line with them, so that all may go forward together evenly.

French planes.

Beginning the Second Day

As we lined up to go over the top the second morning, the battalion looked very small, with less than forty per cent of our original number, and everyone looked worn-out after the nerve racking scenes and experiences of the past twenty-four hours. The men did not possess the spirit they had the previous morning, but their faces showed determination and everyone was ready long before the order. The sanitary *(medical)* men were using German prisoners to carry back our wounded who had been dressed at a first aid station established during the night. As we saw those poor fellows being carried back on stretchers, all wrapped up in bandages and with arms and legs missing, we could hardly wait for revenge.

It was on top of the hill of which we were at the foot, that the machine guns were located which had been used so effectively against us the day before. They had been silent since the early part of the night and we were wondering if they were saving their ammunition to use as we started up after them that morning.

We had some difficulty in arranging squads, as so many specialists had been either killed or wounded. Every soldier cannot operate a machine gun or automatic rifle and, as these various kinds of groups must be placed so that any needed weapon will be available for use against any obstacle; only men who understand them can be used. However, after arranging them as nearly right as possible, we were off.

As we started, our barrage preceded us and as we neared the top of the hill, we could hear the machine guns popping away but they were on another hill across a valley much like the one we had crossed the day before with the exception of the river. There was no firing from the machine guns on the first hill, and as we advanced we found out why. They had all been killed by our artillery, which had kept up a steady fire all night, mowing everything out of our path to make the advance easier.

German POWs carrying wounded Allied soldiers.

Hindered by Barbed Wire

As we reached the crest of the hill and became visible, the machine guns began in earnest from the hill across the valley and our progress was again checked. Up until this time, we had had no barbed wire to contend with, so thoroughly had every inch of ground been swept by our shell fire, but here, just over the top of this hill, was an entanglement about 20 feet wide which had only been partially destroyed, The bullets were whistling rather closely and quite often finding their mark. Everyone was lying in shell holes here and there and the experience of the previous day had taught all to be cautious, but we knew we could not stay there, so one by one we began going forward, running and jumping through the entanglement and down to the valley where it was safe. After we got in the valley, we were out of range and slowly worked our way to the side of the other hill where dead space made it safe. After reaching there, we halted and remained until next day, as it was next to impossible to take the large number of machine guns with our greatly reduced force.

Looking back on the hill we had left, we could see the unfortunate ones hanging on the wires where they had been caught when trying to make their dash to safety.

An Allied soldier who died to liberate France.

Advancing Under Difficulties

It is pretty hard to die on the point of a bayonet, but one at least has the satisfaction of fighting back. Here, we could do absolutely nothing but advance until we fell. The distance between hills was such that we could not locate the Germans who were heavily camouflaged, and all we could do was to advance to the foot and, when our planes came over in the afternoon, give them our location with the panels of jalon and let the artillery shell them all night.

They had no dug-outs to go in and were at our mercy when the big shells fell. Occasionally there would be a concrete pill box, but these were either destroyed or captured after all the others were silenced. We kept going in this manner for five days, each one seeming like years, until on the sixth morning we lay behind a hill, on the opposite side of which lay a village *(Sechault)*. As we went forward and reached the top of the hill, a beautiful plain stretched out before us. Shells were falling all around and the smoke made it difficult to see a great distance, but as far as we could see was level and we were able to distinguish three villages. One was perhaps four miles away and looked to be quite large (perhaps 3,000 population during peace time). Occasionally a burst of smoke would float up showing that our artillery had the range and were trying to drive the soldiers out of it. Another one was about three-fourths of a mile from us, to the right, and forward and into this village, the French troops on our right were already entering. It was evident that there were no Germans in it as they were proceeding without any trouble. The third lay directly in front of us and about one-half mile from the foot of the hill.

Note the multiple stretches of wire; this is also depicted on the battle maps. This is what they looked like for the soldiers who had to get through them; many men did not make it.

HS Fr. File: 577-30.1: Order

American 369th Regiment to Take Sechault

[Editorial Translation]

GENERAL STAFF
G-3
General Order
No. 92

161st DIVISION,
September 28, 1918---24 h.

[Extract]

    I.   Herewith general operations order of the IX Army Corps dated September [27, 1918].
[not attached].
    II.   That order modifies by bringing towards the west the limits of the zone of
action previously assigned to this division * * *
    III.   The primary mission of the division is, if this has not already been accomplished
during the night, to completely occupy the promontory northeast of Signal de Bellevue and
Mont-Cuvelet.

* * * * * *

    IV.   As soon as this has been achieved, the 3 regiments will, first of all, take
necessary measures to begin moving in the general direction of Ferme Les Rosiers and in
the following order: In the lead, center regiment (American 369th Inf.) will seize
Sechault and proceed towards Les Rosiers (Ferme). In echelon, in rear, on the left,
163d Inf. Regt. In echelon, in rear, on the right, 363d Inf. Regt.

* * * * * *

                  LEBOUC,
                  General,
                  Commanding the 161st Inf. Div.

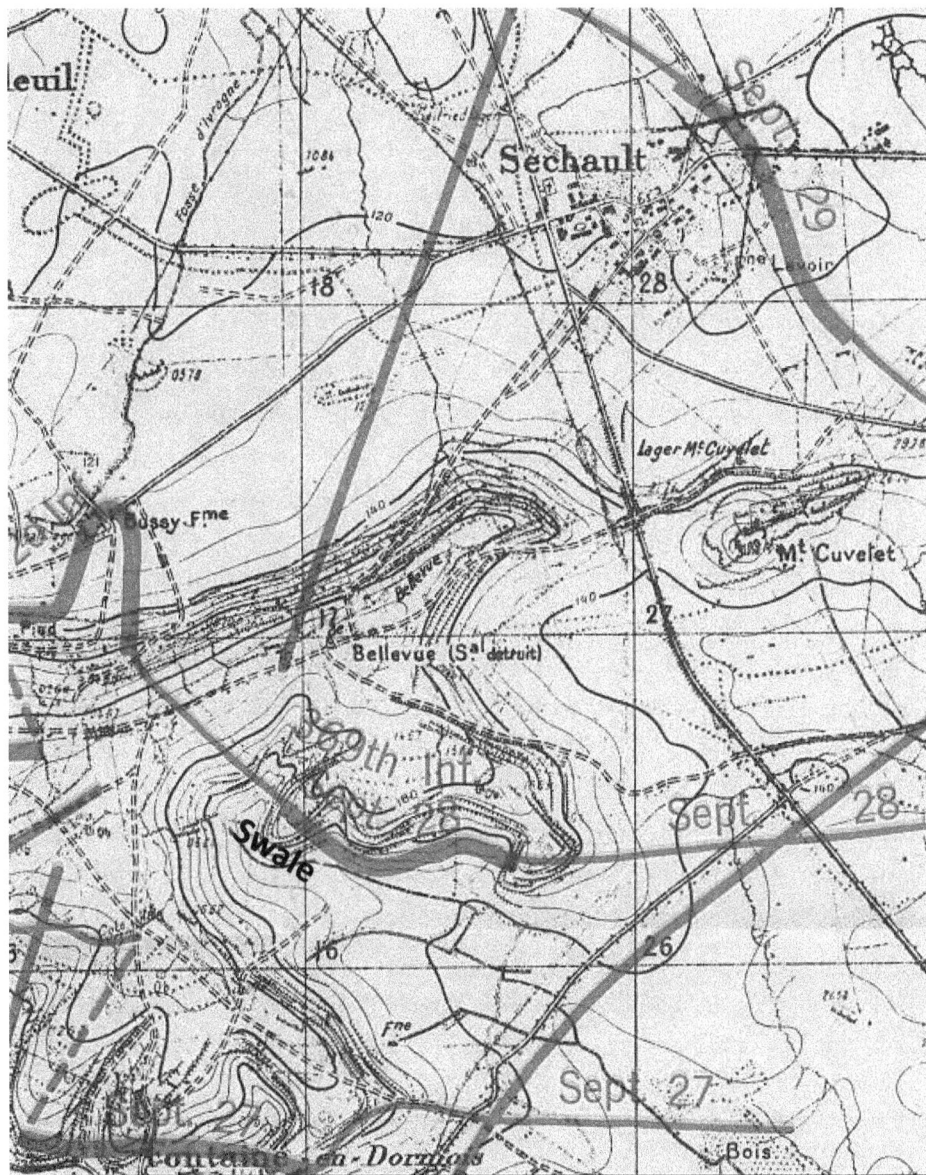

The drive towards Sechault required the capture of the Bellevue heights, forever known thereafter as Snake Hill to the men of the 369th. The swale (dead space) behind the ridgeline provided some shelter from German machine guns and artillery. The men moved forward, across the plain towards the village, which was secured on the 29th, at great cost.

Our barrage was falling between us and the village and everything looked quiet down there. The buildings were in fairly good shape compared with many towns in the war zone. They were, as a matter of fact, about twelve kilometers from the front lines, although we did not realize it at the time. The sense of reckoning time and distance is lost by men in battle.

Hampered by Own Barrage

The order to go forward was given and, as we went forward, it was noticed that this barrage did not move. There was a series of trenches at the foot of the hill, and, as the shelling was so heavy, we took shelter in them, not knowing what was wrong but beginning to think that it was a German barrage, laid down to prevent us from entering the village. The shells were throwing dirt on us as we crouched in the shallow trenches, and just as it began to look pretty bad for us, it was discovered that it was our own barrage and immediately we began sending up red rockets which, at that time (the code changes often) meant, "Your light artillery is falling short." At about this time, machine guns began firing at us from hidden places in the village less than a half mile away. The barrage still fell short and it began to look as If we would soon be released from duty in the trenches. More red rockets were sent up and green ones meaning, "Your heavy artillery is falling short," although there was no heavy artillery doing so. We kept sending up rockets and waiting for results, while machine gun bullets and flying shrapnel carried on.

At last the supply of rockets was gone and then we used three stars which meant, "Lift the barrage, we are going forward." After we had used the last one, we were no better off than before we started. It was then that men saw the advantage of holding on to the rockets, which are usually the first thing thrown away when the load becomes heavy after a long march.

It was possible, being behind the hill, that they did not go high enough to be seen by artillery observers. Sometimes though, when they are seen, they are not heeded, as there are several guns covering the same objective and, when an order of that kind is given, each gun crew thinks that they are firing alright and that it must be one of the others. Consequently no one makes any changes.

More Losses Before Victory

As we could not go forward and bullets were flying too close to stay where we were, it was decided to go back on top of the hill and wait. We were able to follow the trenches and thus we got out without any losses. On the top of this hill, there was a sort of basin about eighty feet across at the top and fifteen or twenty feet deep. The hill gradually sloped from this on three sides and an opening on one side made it easy to get in. What was left of the battalion huddled in this, not knowing what to do.

By dividing the officers up, there was one to each company but, with the exception of one, they were all juniors who had taken the place of the commanders when they had fallen.

We had been travelling six days on our emergency rations and it is needless to say that they had been exhausted some time previous, as there was only enough for two days. While we were wondering what to do, Captain Fish came up with two loaves of bread under his arms and the good news that he had a hundred loaves that he had secured and brought up with men who were in the rear, where they had gone with prisoners. Before he could take the bread from under his arm, it had been taken and eaten by the half-starved men.

We were arranging to send a guide back to show the food detail the way up when a German shell dropped in the hole killing four instantly and wounding three or four so they died within a few minutes, besides gassing and slightly wounding several others. It was decided to wait a few minutes before sending anyone out, but another shell falling in the open side of the basin, killing one man, was sufficient to cause all to move, which we did, going back to the dead space on the other side of the hill.

That afternoon we went forward again and succeeded in taking the town at about six o'clock that evening. Our losses had become so great that it was necessary for another battalion to go forward in front of us and we were placed in reserve, where we remained until the tenth of October.

Village of Sechault, looking east. Bellevue Signal is the high ground at the right. The 369th drove the Germans out of their machine gun nests there, and then crossed the half-mile of open plain to capture the town.
Below: 369th dead, outside of Sechault.

The *369ᵗʰ US Infantry entered the Meuse-Argonne Offensive with approximately 2,700 men. The table below shows the casualties incurred by the unit during the brutal days from September 26th to October 6th. Even though it was pulled back from Sechault, it spent several days at the front, waiting to be rotated to the rear. There were 851 reported casualties, out of 2,700 men, nearly 32% of its force. As the unit rested and refitted, it was joined by both new replacement troops and also with men returning from hospital.*

CASUALTIES, MEUSE-ARGONNE (CHAMPAGNE) OFFENSIVE

		Sept. 16–25	Sept. 26–27	Sept. 28–Oct. 1	Oct. 2–11	Total
369th Inf	W	8	148	480	43	679
	DW	1	4	31	1	37
	K	3	70	52	10	135

STRENGTH OF 93D DIVISION [1]

Units	Aug. 31	Sept. 30	Oct. 31	Nov. 30
369th Inf	2,781	2,328	2,529	2,528
370th Inf	3,179	2,951	2,762	2,906
371st Inf	2,819	2,246	2,230	2,652
372d Inf	2,708	2,826	2,486	2,659

[1] Present with the regiments; does not include absentees.

133

An Instance of Revenge

I shall never forget one occasion when a battalion commander had suffered very heavy losses and his temper gave way when his adjutant was killed. The machine gunner, who had been doing all the damage, either because his ammunition was exhausted or as his only avenue of escape, surrendered. He came forward and was but a few feet from this officer, when he (the officer) whipped out his automatic and killed him. The effect that this had upon any other Germans who may have seen it can easily be imagined.

The effect that it had upon me was anything but pleasant. I was but a few feet away and could distinguish the features of the prisoner. It is easy enough to kill men when they are at a distance great enough to prevent this, but in cases of this kind, it is different and is nothing but heartless, cold blooded murder, forbidden by International Law, every clause of which was broken in the recent struggle.

The officer was 2nd Lt. Harold J. Sargent, of Wisconsin, assigned to Company M of the Third Battalion, killed in action by machine gun fire on September 28, 1918. The officer acting in revenge was Captain, later Major, David L'Esperance, called by his men, the "King Rattler."

2nd Lt. Harold J. Sargent - Major David L'Esperance
& Major Lorillard Spencer, February 19, 1919.

OUT OF THE LINE

Removed From the Drive

We were then taken out of the drive and marched back to billets, behind which the lines had been before we started. Did it seem good to get in a bunk that was made of chicken netting and a couple of army blankets as lousy as lousy could be? I might ask you that, after sleeping for twenty days, with at least eight of them rainy; on the ground with the heavens for a roof, shells falling all about while you tried to sleep, practically no food and nothing about you but dead and dying and the horrible stench that prevails on a battle field in the hot September sun? I shall never forget those fields covered with their silent, motionless figures clad in the khaki of the United States, the horizon blue of France and the field gray of the Germans. Many of these bodies lay for ten days in the hot sun before the pioneers, sappers and bombers, etc., came along to bury them and to eat and sleep in such a place was not at all pleasant.

Did I sleep that first night? All I can say is that Rip Van Winkle, with his great love for sleep under even normal conditions, would sleep through all eternity after an experience like that. I slept in proportion.

Discomfort of Suspicion

After resting three or four days, we were taken in motor trucks to the cleanest village I saw in France; at least it appeared that way to me. We stayed there about ten days and almost everyone was anxious to get out of it. It may seem strange that we should want to get away from such an ideal spot, but we had only been there a couple of days when one of the civilians reported the loss of a watch. Our major *(David L'Esperance),* who detested anyone who stole or who knew of it and would not tell, ordered the battalion to fall in with full equipment. No one knew what was up but supposed we were moving again. We were marched out in a field near the town and while we stood there listening to his speech a guard was posted around us.

NCO conducting roll call, October 1918 in France.

He said that a watch had been stolen and that we should not enter the town again until the thief had been found. As the barns had plenty of hay in them, which was much nicer than lying on the ground in the cold October rains after all we had been through, it was, he said, to everybody's interest to find the guilty party. I have reasons to believe that many French people, after finding out the liberal ways of Americans, and being paid for things they claimed were stolen without question, worked this "gag" to the limit. Be it as it may, we never entered the town again and were happy when we entrained for Belfort.

Traveling to Belfort

The trip to Belfort was quite a long one, taking about fifty hours. The weather was quite chilly, being the latter part of October, but as we were given our bale of straw for each car, we were fairly comfortable in our "side door Pullmans."

Once or twice during the trip, we stopped at coffee stations and were given coffee and sandwiches by the Red Cross. On one occasion, us we were jolting along, we came to a sudden stop about midnight and coffee was passed the entire length of the train. It had enough cognac in it to give one a slight feeling of warmth, but, as a whole I think the men would have preferred to have been left asleep, as it is quite a hard matter to get asleep in one of the French troop trains. During the day everyone wants to view the scenery, and as soon as darkness prevents this, singing is in order. This usually continues well until midnight, and once awakened, it takes several hours to get all hands quieted down again.

Upon detraining, we passed through the center of the city on our ten kilometer hike to our billets.

Area of the Vosges Mountains occupied by the 369th.

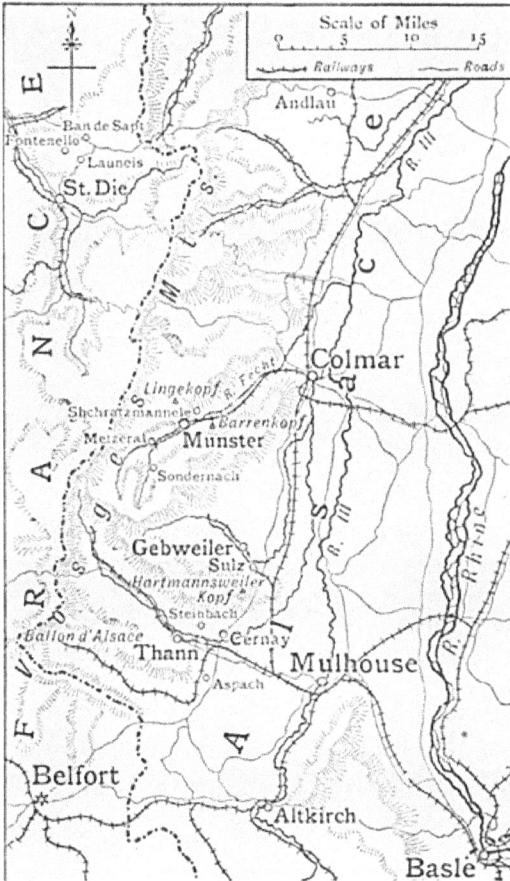

Belfort City Well Protected

Belfort is a beautiful city of several thousand inhabitants and is protected by a large wall which encircles it, in addition to the many forts which located on the near-by hills. Large gates operated by machinery open and close the various entrances to the town. It would be a very hard city to capture, and no one knows this any better than Germany, who sacrificed 35,000 men just outside the city during the Franco-Prussian war of 1870-71 in trying to capture it.

We were very glad when we finally reached a small village and were assigned billets, and everyone had visions of a few weeks' rest in comfortable quarters.

No one seemed to know just what we were going to do, but it had been rumored that we would get two or three months behind the lines, as was customary with all French troops after a long campaign. Then, too, it was found that the colored troops of the French colonies did not do well in the trenches during the extremely cold weather, and were usually taken to southern France and used for other purposes during the winter.

We had had enough of war for a while and felt confident that we would see no more of it for a time, at least. This was the general impression of officers and men.

Disillusion of Troops Bitter

That night, I was awakened at 11 o'clock and given an order requiring all officers and first sergeants to report to battalion headquarters at once. I got up and, in the pouring rain, summoned the officers of my company. Reporting at headquarters, I found that we were to enter another sector at once, leaving there at 7 o'clock the next morning *(October 16th)*. I think the hardest job I had during the war was the one that night, of going and telling the men to be up at 5:30 next morning for breakfast and ready to fall in at 6:00 with full equipment, as we had a short march to get to the place where we were to meet the camions that were to carry us. About the only ones who welcomed this news were some of the officers and enlisted men, who had come to us to fill the place of those killed and wounded; surely none of us who had so lately come out of battle, some whose wounds had not yet fully healed.

Sent to Alsace

We had a ride of about six hours and travelled only about thirty kilometers, owing to the mountains which we had to cross and finally brought up in Moosch, a small village in Alsace, which lies in a long valley alongside the Vosges Mountains.

Here we found everything much different than anything we had seen in our travels about France. Alsace and Lorraine are beautiful countries, and when one sees them he doesn't wonder that so many lives have been given for the possession of such a rich country. Nearly everyone is interested to know a little about the two countries that are called the "night-mare of Europe," and I shall mention a few facts of interest that I have been able to gather.

The Coveted Provinces

In 1881, the Kaiser, in speaking of this country, gave utterance to these words: "Germany would leave her eighteen army corps and her forty-two million people on the field of battle, rather than surrender a single stone of the territory won in 1870."

They are located at the northeast corner of France. Together they are about as large as Yellowstone National Park, or the size of six Iowa counties. The soil is the most fertile to be found in central Europe. The hills are richly wooded with fir, oak and beech, as well as other varieties. Corn, flax, tobacco, grapes and various fruits are grown. The great wealth however, is in the minerals; iron, lead, copper, coal, rock salt and even silver are there. Manufacturers of cotton and linen are plentiful.

After the Franco-Prussian war in 1870-71, a provision in the Treaty of Frankfort allowed those who wished to cross the line into France to go. Of course, this meant leaving their homes, their farms, their old neighbors and everything else they could not take along. More than a year was given for this, and, on the last day of grace, one author says: "All those who had means of transportation rode in carts, wagons, carriages, running over the back roads. Whole families drove on their cattle. Old men dragged themselves on, leaning on the shoulders of young women, who bore at the breast new born children. Sick men, who wished not to die German, were carried bodily that they might draw the last breath on the frontier of-Nancy and thank heaven to die on French soil."

Then the Germans tried to blot out all traces of France. The French language was forbidden in schools, on advertisements, or even on tombs. Police and secret service men watched the inhabitants and men were imprisoned for any demonstration that exalted France. I have been told by people who lived there during this period that children could not even go to school with a hair ribbon on containing the French colors. All French flags that could be found were destroyed. Occasionally, one was so well hidden that it could not be found.

It is said that when General Joffre and the French army entered Alsace in August 1914 the joy of the people knew no bounds. French flags that had been hidden away for forty-three years were brought out, and such scones of rejoicing have rarely been witnessed.

As might be expected, when the French army was driven out of Alsace later on, the people suffered untold misery. Thousands were condemned to prison for years for the awful crime of maintaining their French sentiments. A single word that reflected upon what Germany had done in any way would send some to prison.

The number of women condemned to prison was enormous, for the women of Alsace were more outspoken and less respectful to

Germans than the men. Women of the noble class filled the prisons. One woman with tear-dimmed eyes was brought to a jailor, who said: "Do not weep, madam, you will find yourself in excellent company. Our house is the only one in which you can speak French with impunity." It is said that thirty thousand of these people were deported into Germany and their lot was worse than death.

After we had been assigned billets, and as soon as we had laid our equipment away, we began to look about the town.

554. La Grande Guerre 1914-15
Haute-Alsace. — Vue de MOOSCH. — Vallée de THANN   A. R.

American Girl in Store Near Front

I chanced to go into a small store where a sign announced English cigarettes for sale, and to my surprise and delight, I was greeted by the proprietress who said ''Good Afternoon" in excellent English. Upon inquiry, I found that she was an American girl whose home was on Seventh Ave., New York City, before her marriage to a Frenchman. Soon after their marriage, they had left America and opened this little store in Alsace. When war was declared, he had responded to the call to arms and she, being unable to return to America, as was her desire, was forced to remain in Moosch and so we found her running the little store as a means of livelihood. Her husband was killed and she was waiting for the war to cease, so that she might return to her home in New York.

During our conversation, I asked her how far we were from the front, and she coolly replied that it was but two miles. At first I could not believe her, as the village was in a better state of preservation than any I had ever seen ten miles behind the lines in the various parts of the front that I had been located in. There were no signs that would indicate that a shell had even burst in the town. She assured me that I would find fighting enough "up on the hill," as she called it, and I found out later that she knew what she was talking about.

Alsace Villages Spared

In Alsace, the French and Germans have intermarried, and, for the most part, they speak "Alsatian," which is a combination of the two languages. The sympathies of these people were, I think, nearly equally divided at the beginning of the war and, in many instances, brothers, fathers and sons, etc., joined opposing forces. As French people are living behind the German lines in the nearby villages and vice versa, these villages are not shelled by either side. All the inhabitants are provided with gas masks as a precautionary measure, however.

Mountain Sector Dangerous

On the day following our arrival, we entered the trenches on the top of the "Grosse Bleichen" *(Grand Balloon in English),* the highest point of the Vosges Mountains, which rises to an altitude of 4,672 feet.

All supplies had to be taken to the trenches on pack mules and about five hours were required for troops with equipment, although the distance was little more than two miles. It was much colder on top of the mountains, even in October, than one would think from the valley below, and while it was very pleasant down in the villages, we had very heavy frosts each night up in the trenches.

The artillery of our division were preparing for a long vacation as they would not shell the towns and the only firing, excepting rifles and grenades, was by the small caliber cannon of the "mountain artillery," which were transported by pack mules.

We were told by the French that this was regarded as the worst sector of the entire front, as the infantry was constantly making raids using grenades for their barrages instead of artillery, and men were captured every day by ambuscades. The dense foliage of the firs made trenches or breast-works unnecessary and the only fortifications were where the men slept. Around these places, stonewalls were built and resembled old time stockades.

The German troops opposing us were men who were skilled in woodcraft and were largely men who had always lived in these mountains. They would come over in the night and lie along the paths and when anyone would pass the following day would capture them and take them back the following night. This had been done with such success that French general headquarters issued an order that not less than eight men travel in the paths as far back as battalion headquarters, and then every man had to be armed with a loaded rifle, cocked and carried under the arm much the same as the hunter carries a shotgun when hunting.

Germany's Methods of Checking Advances

About this time the Allies were making offensives along the entire front, hammering first at one point and then at another.

Germany had no superfluous manpower and when one of these drives would start, all her available men would be rushed to that point to check it. They would no sooner get to one point than a fresh drive launched somewhere else would claim their attention. In this way, they were started backward along the larger part of the line.

Their rear guard action was wonderful. In every conceivable place, they would have machine gun nests so heavily camouflaged that their discovery was impossible until within a few rods of them. They would have an adequate supply of ammunition and were experts in its use. As the main army would fall back, these would be left behind, sacrificed; to enable the main body to retire and take back as much as possible while they hampered the advance of the Allies.

It has been said that in many instances these men have been found chained to their guns. This may have been so, but I have seen a great many dead gunners lying by their guns when we have been advancing and none were ever chained. My experience leads me to believe that chaining was not necessary, as they rarely gave up except when their supply of ammunition was exhausted. They were led to believe that, if taken, they would be killed, and knowing that a like fate awaited them if they returned to their main army, there was nothing to do but die at their post.

To prove to them that they wore misled was the reason that all Allied troops were instructed to conspicuously take those captured to the rear and, in some cases, small groups would be sent alone.

Undrilled Men Victims in Drive

The heavy casualties suffered by the Allies from this Hun method was unavoidable, as attacking troops are exposed and moving and attacked troops are quiet and concealed.

An incident occurred while we were in the Vosges Mountains which clearly showed the use of thorough training before one should enter the trenches. Troops were being rushed over as fast as possible to fill gaps caused by these repeated drives and we received a number of men, some of whom had only been in the service thirty days. We were badly in need of men, as we were holding positions with many less than we should and were forced to put them in without the several weeks' instruction customarily given.

I instructed men in the use of the rifle and gas mask, while we were in Alsace, who were in the first line trenches thirty days from the date they were inducted into the service and who received all their instructions relative to warfare within a period of twenty-four hours prior to facing the well-drilled soldiers of Germany.

Wherever possible, these men were so sandwiched in between seasoned troops that they learned many things in the first few days, but one of our groups, which had an unusually large number of green men in it, was attacked the day following their entry into the lines, and one officer and five men were killed in broad daylight, a thing that could not have happened with well-trained troops. *(Lt. Elmer Bucher, Privates Lake Anderson, John Honaker and Dave Livis, all KIA, Pvt. John McAllister, severely wounded.)*

These men were absolutely helpless, although surrounded by all kinds of defensive weapons, and made the supreme sacrifice simply because they had not been taught to defend themselves.

BUCHER, ELMER ERNEST (Deceased)   CARROLL COUNTY
  First lieutenant, Company C, 369th Infantry, 93d Division
  Croix de Guerre with silver star (France). Order No. 12.184
"D", December 9, 1918, General Headquarters, French Armies of the East: A brave and zealous officer. He was killed on October 28, 1918, while encouraging his men to resist. Gave a magnificent example of devotion.

  Record. Born November 8, 1884, Michigantown; son of Samuel and Sarah Catherine (Boyer) Bucher. Salesman, Delphi. Entered service May 12, 1917, Fort Benjamin Harrison. Training: Fort Benjamin Harrison; Camp Taylor, Ky.; Camp Sherman, Ohio. Assigned to Company C, 335th Infantry; transferred to Company C, 369th Infantry. Second lieutenant, August 15, 1917; first lieutenant, December 31, 1917. Overseas September 4, 1918. Killed in action October 28, 1918, in Alsace. Buried in Masonic Cemetery, Delphi.

ON LEAVE

Permission Leave

A few days prior to the signing of the armistice, our regimental commander was notified that a leave area had been selected to which "permissionaires" of the regiment might be sent.

I was among the first seventy who were selected to go, and, on the afternoon of November 8th, left the trenches and reported at headquarters where the detachment was to assemble. That evening, we were issued two days' travel rations and also new clothing, as what we had was not in very good condition after being in the trenches some time. It is needless for me to add that they were up to trench life requirements in regards to cooties.

We were to take a train at 5:30 the following morning, but our French guide and interpreter was late and we were forced to walk nine miles and then take a narrow gauge railway that ran over the mountains to Bussang, where we got a main line train that afternoon.

Our train was what is known as a "permissionaire" train and only carries soldiers going on permission. These trains collect the soldiers near the front and carry them to what is known as a regulating station. These stations were built during the war and are for the sole purpose of aiding soldiers to travel when on leave and helping the government keep in touch with troops.

Entraining Soldiers on Furlough

As we arrived at one of these regulating stations, we saw hundreds of soldiers already there waiting for trains. We rushed into the enclosure as everybody was in a hurry, in order to get comfortable seats in the next train. The various buildings in the enclosure included, besides the regulating station itself, large waiting rooms where one could sleep if he had to wait overnight and a large canteen where almost any kind of a meal could be purchased. Bread could he bought, provided you had the essential bread tickets, as well as wine, which sells very well, as every French soldier replenishes his stock at every available opportunity.

The French soldier and his canteen are inseparable, and I never saw one carry water.

As the troops pass through the station, their passes are stamped and their names, regiment, etc., taken; and no one can get on a train on the other side unless his pass has been duly stamped.

Once on this side, however, you find trains going to all the large cities of France and it is only necessary to know what large city your destination is near to get there with all possible speed (which is very slow), as these are through trains and carry nothing but soldiers. To see the enormous crowds that pass through these stations each day, one would think that there could be none on duty at the front, but, upon considering the many million in uniform, you soon realize that this is a very small per cent of them.

The first eighteen months of the war, no French soldiers were permitted to go home under any circumstance, but from then until the close of the war, they were given from seven to ten days every four months.

The Day of the Armistice

We left the regulating station on Sunday afternoon, and the following morning at 8:00, our train stopped to change engines. It had no sooner stopped than everyone in the train began yelling at the top of their voices. We seventy Americans did not know what was the cause of all the excitement for a few minutes, but were soon told by one of the Frenchmen that the war was over. As our train stood there, the entire population turned out to have a look at the soldiers. They acted more like insane people than anything else and we, who had been in the trenches so long and had begun to doubt if it would ever end, were forced to believe that something must have happened to make these poor, suffering people act like little children at play after more than four years of war with all its suffering, of which America knows nothing.

They had assembled at the station as soon as we arrived to pay homage to us seventy Americans and to gaze upon part of a triumphant army.

All that day, as we passed through village after village, the same scenes met our eyes. No work was carried on anywhere. Every factory closed and wine and champagne flowed like water.

It was hard for us to believe, and, while we were forced to do it, we could not remove the thought that when we returned we would find things as we had left them.

Chateau-Thierry

That day we passed through Chateau-Thierry and the scenes that met our gaze were such as would make the most hardened veteran shudder. The country through there is quite level, with now and then a knoll, and although no Germans had been there since July, their marks still remained and will for a long time.

The villages are all destroyed. Occasionally one sees a house that has not fallen but the shell holes have ruined it. For miles on either side of the track are the graves of those who fell and here and there they are marked with a rifle and helmet.

On the south-eastern side and less than a quarter of a mile from the railroad station is a grave about fifteen feet by fifteen feet and in the center is a post on which hangs a German helmet denoting that it is filled with Germans. There, as everywhere else, you would see bottles sticking neck down in the graves. This is an unofficial way of leaving some mark of identification. It is usually done by a comrade who writes any bit of information at hand and, being put in a bottle, it will keep indefinitely.

Enjoying Armistice Celebration and Vacation

Tuesday morning, we arrived at St. Malo, a seaport town on the northwestern coast of France. We were met by an M.P. (military police) who guided us to the provost marshal's office. Here everyone registered and had his permission stamped, and our furlough began.

These leave areas were selected with the greatest care, so that the soldier might enjoy his few days' vacation to the fullest and go back to his command as well as when he went away, instead of the wreck he would be were he allowed to tour France at will, unprotected against the many forms of evil which are to be found in many of the cities, and to which soldiers are an easy prey.

All the hotels are at the disposal of the government, and we were given tickets at the provost marshal's which were good for seven days' board at the designated hotel. After being given our tickets and a long lecture as to how we should conduct ourselves, we went to our quarters as it was time for dinner.

Soon after dinner, I was called upon by an M.P. who wanted to know if any of the men were lousy. Needless to say we were, for the changing of our clothes had done little good and the afternoon was spent in bathing and receiving new clothes again.

That night, we took part in an enormous parade which must have included every inhabitant of the town, as well as the 3,000 troops visiting there. The Kaiser was shot, burned and hung in effigy, and we did not get to bed before 11:30.

I cannot describe the feeling we experienced in once more sleeping in an "honest to goodness" bed, and will not attempt it any further than to say that not one in seven men got up for breakfast. The theaters of the city were free to all who wore khaki, and a Y.M.C.A. hut furnished all sorts of entertainment for the men. The hut was formerly a large gambling house and was an ideal building for the "Y." There was always something going on, dancing every afternoon, and shows every night, also excursions every day to the various interesting points nearby. It was very amusing to see the boys struggle to get a partner for a dance. This is not to be wondered at, since there were about 3,000 new boys there every seven days, and only twelve girls who were hired for this purpose. Just before the orchestra would start a selection, arm bands would be put on the arms of those who wished to dance. There were twelve each of the many colors and, at the blow of a whistle, one color would dash for the floor, grab a partner and lay all earthly cares aside for sixty seconds, when the whistle would again blow and another rush on the floor.

52 St-MALO - Le Casino et l'Hôtel Franklin

On Furlough at St. Malo

The topic of every conversation was the signing of the armistice and everyone wore a happy smile. Each day, the beach would be filled with soldiers, and, as they looked westward toward the land of their dreams, they knew that it would not be long before dreams would be realities for already the papers were telling of the plans for immediate demobilization.

It was hard for us to believe that it was really over, and almost everyone half expected to find it the same when we returned.

The time for my group to leave St. Malo came all too quickly, and at the set time we reported to the R.T.O. (railroad transportation officer) and there, along with about five hundred others, had our permissions stamped, received two days travel rations and our furlough was over.

At 5:30 p.m. our train left and as we passed from under the train shed, which is seen at every large station, we bade farewell to St. Malo and the Brittany Leave Area where we spent the pleasantest seven days of our time while in the A. E. F.

The Return Trip

On our return trip, we passed within three miles of Paris and had a glimpse of the city but it was useless for us to try to get there as M.Ps. were placed everywhere about it to keep soldiers out. Paris was the Mecca of all U.S. troops, and for many months no enlisted men were allowed, except those who were in the hospitals there. Many officers were arrested who stole in as they were going from one point to another. Had it not been for this, we could easily have stopped off for a day or two, as time of travel is not included in the furloughs.

When we first arrived in France, before the military police system had been so thoroughly established, one could get off at any station and spend a day or two and then continue his journey. Many of the boys have spent a couple of weeks in travelling a distance that could have been covered in one or two days.

It became so that at any small town you might want to get off at, an M.P. would find out if you had a pass, and if you had no authority for being there, you were quickly started on your way. A French soldier with whom I became intimately acquainted told me how, when he would get a ten day leave, he would, at the expiration of his time report and get his permission stamped and return home for a few extra days before actually starting to join his regiment.

French Prisoners Released

Our two rations were gone when we reached Favresse, our regulating station, and we were hungry after our two-day ride. There was a little money left in the crowd and we bought some food. We could get no train out until the small hours of the morning and time hung heavily on us. There were a few French prisoners who had been released by Germany, and were waiting for trains to their homes. It was enough to touch a heart of stone to see the haggard faces which plainly showed how they had fared. They had no money, but they did not want for food as everybody was only too anxious to give them food. They wore the old worn out clothing of German soldiers and each one had a large white band on his arm. They had been released at the signing of the armistice, and without money or food, had to get back to their own country as best they could, many from prison camps a long distance from the border.

Seeking the Regiment

The following night, we reached Epinal and being very hungry we went to the headquarters of a detachment of U.S. soldiers stationed there, and secured some food, after which we got a train to Bussany, from which we had to go the rest of the journey by narrow gauge. It was about 11:00 p m. when we arrived, and freezing cold. There were no trains going over the mountains until the next morning so we made ourselves comfortable in a building nearby.

When we got up the next morning, we found ourselves up against a serious proposition. The only train going over the mountain had gone and we did not feel like "hiking it" without food, as it was at least ten miles to where we had left the regiment, and half this distance was up the mountains. We did not know whether we would find the regiment there or not, but without money or food, we realized that we must soon find them or starve.

Just when things looked worst, a Y.M.C.A. secretary came along and after much persuasion we succeeded in getting them to take us over the mountains. Arriving on the other side, we found that our regiment had gone forward in the Amy of Occupation, but, as the Supply Company had not left yet, we succeeded in getting some food and continued our journey after getting the name of the place they were located at.

I shall never forget that hike nor the many things of interest I saw on the way, as I went from what had been "No Man's Land" but a few days before to the Rhine River, where the regiment was stationed.

As I came to the ruined villages near where the line had been, I could see that some of the houses were occupied and here and there an old man or woman would be looking at what I supposed had once been their home, but which had not a shingle left to cover them. The roads were lined with these old people who were going back to their homes. Where the road went across "No Man's Land," the barbed wire had been removed and shell holes filled up. The German trenches, dug-outs, etc., were practically the same as ours. They had, at the point where I crossed the line, a live wire which ran along in front of their positions, to electrocute any of our men who might get too inquisitive.

Farther back, I found the villages decorated with home-made French and American flags. Some of them were made of paper, and in one place I recall seeing an American flag with eight stars and ten stripes, but it was sufficient to show that their spirit was with us. No matter what the feelings of these people may have been in that period from 1871 until the war, they are now filled with hatred toward Germany because of their sufferings during the recent conflict. They were deprived of the crops that they raised and nearly everything was taken away from them to the point of starvation in many cases.

OCCUPATION

Ingenuity of Germans

At one point I passed through the edge of a forest and there camouflaged by trees, were miles and miles of railroad switches upon which rolling stock and material was safe from observation. The most elaborate dug-outs I have seen were in this wood. They were one room affairs about 12 by 14 feet, and had white polished walls such as are found in the American home. The roofs were level with the ground and were of concrete, about three feet thick.

The furnishings of these had evidently been in keeping with the rest, judging by the pictures hanging on the walls and the few remaining pieces of furniture. They had, without doubt, been the headquarters of high officers. Souvenir hunters would have found rich pickings here, for almost everything imaginable was to be found. They had taken the larger part but a great deal was left in their haste to evacuate.

Fowl Scarce on the Rhine

I finally reached my company, which was billeted in a small town called Fessenheim, about two miles from the Rhine and not far from the Swiss border.

I stayed in a room that was used as a meat market one day each week and was greatly surprised when market day came to see the way business was conducted. The meat arrived the night before, brought from a neighboring town on a small wagon drawn by a dog, and the amount would not exceed sixty pounds. This was a week's supply for a town of at least 300 inhabitants.

The following morning, the people would form a line in front of the door and, as soon as the butcher, who was a lady, arrived, the business of the week began. No one could purchase without meat tickets and only a very small amount then. I have seen one person buy a piece which would weigh between one and two pounds, but do not know how many were in the family. Many times the meat is all sold before the end of the line is reached and in that case they get none and their only hope is to get there earlier next time.

The half loaf of bread which we were issued daily would get almost anything that these starving people had, and many of the boys secured valuable pieces of jewelry, etc., by depriving themselves of bread for one day,

According to the terms of the armistice, all Alsatian soldiers were to be released within thirty days, and every day a few would be seen going to their homes. Some of our men who were wounded in the second battle of the Marne *(Meuse-Argonne)* came back to us while we were stationed here, and the sight of these returned [enemy] troops filled them with anger and they would have given anything for the privilege of getting even.

The river was too shallow for navigation at this point, being quite near its source and we had very little to do. Companies would go up and remain for forty-eight hours patrolling the bank and be relieved by other companies. We could see the Germans doing likewise on the opposite bank, but conversations and crossings were strictly forbidden. We were guarded against surprises and had been from the moment actual fighting ceased.

The Trenches on November 11th

The men of my regiment who were in the trenches received word between 9:00 and 10:00 a.m. that fighting would cease at 11:00 and the joy that that message brought can only be realized by those who were there.

The men could not believe it and decided not to be caught napping. On the very minute, the Germans began climbing out of their trenches yelling like mad, and came over to our lines giving the boys cigarettes, cigars and souvenirs. Our men remained at their posts until they were sure that the Germans had no weapons. Then, and not until then, did they join in the celebration. And such a celebration as those war-sick men had, who had been away from homes and families, amid death and devastation for months and years is beyond the writer to describe. The Germans invited our boys over and many of them accepted and went over and spent an hour or two visiting their enemies of a few hours ago, who were better friends because of the sufferings and privations all had shared alike. Several of the Germans spoke English and a good time was enjoyed by all who accepted the invitation. The nights that followed were far different from what they had been. All the rockets in the trenches were used up and singing extended into the early hours of the morning. Then came the orders to go forward and every precaution was taken lest they be caught in a Hun trap. Our division went forward with their advance guard out and ready for instant defense should occasion demand.

American soldiers celebrate news of the Armistice.

While we were on the Rhine, we were so situated as to hold off any ordinary attack the Germans might make; our artillery, machine guns, etc. being all ready to start firing.

About the middle of December, the order came for all American troops who were brigaded with the French, and in the French Army of Occupation to be released, and, in compliance with that order we turned our faces west for the first time since 1917 and started on our journey homeward.

Ungersheim, Alsace-Lorraine, December 12, 1918
Then – and Now

HOMEWARD BOUND

Starting for Home

We started back toward home we could not go fast enough and men who had been suffering from various ills were magically healed.

After a one-day hike, we were held in a village for three or four days and during this time everybody was souvenir hunting among the German peasants. The German war cross ("iron cross") was readily selling at $10.00. After leaving this village, we went to a little village on the outskirts of Belfort and remained there during the holidays. The weather was very cold and the ground was covered with snow.

We had received no clothing for a long time as the uncertainty of our remaining on the Rhine had prevented any being shipped to us from the Quartermaster Corps and although some of the men were practically barefooted and almost without clothing, they would not give up as they were told that should they go to a hospital they would be transferred to labor battalions and might possibly stay another year in France. It was only when a man could hardly stand up that he would give in and be evacuated.

Each day we would drill a little while and to see the men marching with their bare feet in the snow when the shoes were worn out reminded one very much of Revolutionary days when they had no well-stocked quartermaster and the unlimited resources that we have been boasting of since the war began.

During the first week of January, we received orders to proceed to Le Mans and the morning following its receipt found us marching toward "Mor villars" where we entrained. But we could not forget our suffering at Chautenois; exceeded only during battles; nor will it ever be forgotten by those who were there.

The trip to Le Mans was undoubtedly the pleasantest of any that we had on French railroads. At least four times during our forty-eight hour ride we stopped for coffee, sandwiches, cigarettes and candy. And such excellent candy too. It was impossible to get good candy in France owing to scarcity of sugar. Realizing the American doughboys' longings for sweets resulted in the establishing of an enormous candy factory by the A.E.F. Each soldier was supposed to get a half-pound package every ten days. We had been neglected somewhat in getting our share and it seemed as if they wanted to give us all that we had missed.

These little favors were insignificant when compared with the fact that we were going home. Sixty minutes of every one of the forty-eight hours we were riding, one could hear singing in some of the cars and no one objected.

Arrival at Le Mans

Arriving at Le Mans, we were assigned to quarters in a small tent city which had been prepared for receiving home bound troops. Le Mans is an inland town and so situated as to be quite easily reached from any part of France except the south.

It was here that the Armies were assembled before going to the front. Practically all troops passed through to the front. Immediately upon the signing of the armistice and the backward movement of troops, it was turned into an embarkation and forwarding camp through which a large per cent of the home-ward bound army would pass.

Troops coming in from the front are kept in the tents until they pass through the delousing plant. After being deloused they are assigned barracks and thus one part of the camp is kept clean and the other dirty as the army passes on. After spending one night in the tents we were taken to the delouser. After we had laid down all our equipment, we were ready to go through the "mill" as it is called. Entering a long building, you begin undressing as you pass through, throwing one garment here, one there until—well, you get rid of all your clothing just as you find you are at the end of the building and just outside the bathroom door through which you are quickly hurried by the men who are stationed there, to see that things are properly done. As you step in the bathroom, you are given a good covering of something resembling paper hangers' paste. You then get under a shower and for three minutes lukewarm water is turned on very sparingly. A generous amount of cold water follows and half freezing, you rush on to the next room where you receive a new supply of clothing. This is sometimes new but too often it is old clothing that has been sterilized. It is a long building with an aisle in the center and on either side the clothing is stacked. You do not stop but yell your size as you pass by. After going into another room, you dress and step out into the world free from the worst curse that ever afflicted anyone.

There is another "mill" at Le Mans. This one is for the issuing of equipment and is operated in much the same way. When you come out of this mill, you have all the equipment of a soldier including gas mask and helmet, which, although the war was over were issued because they had to be brought back and several thousand troops could be brought over in the space that they would have taken if shipped in cases.

All records had to be correct before any unit could leave the camp and this necessitates lots of hard work by the clerical force as records are apt to get mixed up considerably at the front.

1/28/19. Brest Camp Pontanezen from Marine Tower.

Off for Brest.

We finally surmounted all obstacles and were ready to start the next lap of our journey. This was the trip to Brest where we were embark and, as we marched to the railroad siding and saw the train that was to take us, our joy knew no bounds, for there on the track was a train made up entirely of American box cars drawn by an American locomotive and mid-way of the train, a flat car with the specially designed A.E.F. troop kitchen. The odor which came from it assured us that we would not be hungry on the journey. No one who has not ridden on a French troop train could appreciate a sight of this kind. We could hardly believe our eyes but the letters: U.S.A. stood out so plainly against the background of French gray that we could not doubt it.

The trip from Le Mans to Brest is an all-American one, and the road is known as the American shuttle. The track had been laid by American engineers and is operated by "men in khaki" for the transportation of U.S. troops and supplies. The writer does not know the length of the shuttle, but twenty-four hours is required to make the trip.

The cars are somewhat smaller than those in the United States but comfortably accommodate fifty-six men and equipment. Each car is provided with two lanterns and a toilet, something not found very often in day coaches over there; and with no chance for the wind to blow through, they are very comfortable.

Arrival at Brest

We arrived in Brest about 8:00 p m. and recognized it, although it was very dark, as soon as we stepped in the mud.

There is mud enough there to last several years even without rain, and since there is no prospect of drought, the inhabitants have no worry in this respect.

We detrained and were taken under a large shed to await orders as we did not know whether we were to embark or go into camp. At the end of about two hours we were ordered to go into camp which was on the hill above the town about three miles distant.

It was about 3:00 a.m. when we were finally assigned to quarters which were in the muddiest section of the muddiest place on earth. In going to our tents, one was compelled to walk in mud from eight to sixteen inches deep. The inside of the tents was little better and into this we were forced to lie down and sleep with nothing but our blankets which were in keeping with the surroundings when we were ordered up for reveille two and one-half hours later. We remained in these tents four or five days before being deloused again and given barracks.

Unidentified MPs addressing black troops at a rest area.

Much has been said of the camp at Brest, as it was during the early part of 1919 and everyone knows how the troops were forced to suffer while waiting for transportation until the War Department effected certain changes. The writer read many of the articles that appeared in the press from time to time, none of which exaggerated the true conditions.

All organizations were kept at work, and all details were forced to march at attention. Men were called down if caught talking while at work, and it was not unusual to stand in line for an hour waiting for mess as four and five thousand men were fed at each kitchen. Many times men would miss meals rather than stand in line for perhaps an hour in the pouring rain waiting for it.

During this time it was necessary to stand at attention and if anyone should violate this rule, that detachment would be reported by one of the numerous M.Ps. and the entire organization would be placed at the bottom of the sailing list.

Bidding France Good-bye

Our conduct was such however, that we finally received sailing orders and on the first day of February, we embarked. The hike down the hill was made in absolute silence and at attention. We were told that troops had been taken back to camp after reaching the dock because there had been talking on the way down. At the dock we went aboard small boats which carried us into the harbor where we boarded the "La France," the largest passenger boat of France. Sunday, Feb. 2d, at 2:20 p.m. we lifted anchor and bade good-bye to France.

Men of the 369th arriving on *SS LaFrance*, February, 1919.

COMING HOME

Homeward Bound and the Arrival

The trip across the ocean was very pleasant. There were no submarines to fear. Lights were kept burning all night and one could walk about the decks and even talk without fear of court-martial. The topic most discussed was the arrival home, and when we slid into harbor Sunday morning, everybody was out trying to get a look at the Statue of Liberty, which German propaganda said had been destroyed. It was in place, however, and a large number of the boys vowed they were looking at its face for the last time, unless it turned around,

We were met by the Mayor's Committee of Welcome out in the bay, and newspapers, candy and cigarettes were thrown to us by the committee. Arriving at the pier, we were quickly taken by ferry to the Long Island Railroad, where we entrained tor Camp Upton, but in the small space of time between debarking and entraining, we received more tobacco, cigarettes and candy than during our entire time in France.

As we boarded the train, we were each given a large cake, and many baskets of sandwiches were passed through the train. Did it seem good to see New York? I'll say so, and it will always be remembered as the happiest day of our lives, when we recalled the death and destruction that had been all about us; the many comrades who had looked forward to this homecoming until the grim reaper had come along and decided otherwise.

To look back made one feel like coming from death into life, and, happy as we were, we would have been far happier could we have forgotten the awful scenes left behind on the sacred soil of France which serves as a last resting place for many of America's sons.

Homeward-bound; men of the 369th aboard transport ship, 1919.

Good News Learned at Camp

Arriving at Camp Upton, we were put in comfortable quarters, and on Monday we were told that we would be discharged on Friday. It was too good to believe for we had been so long with the French that we had become accustomed to their slow and easy-going manner.

However, on Tuesday morning, the process of demobilization began and everybody began planning for the trip home on Friday.

Routine of Disbanding

It is not as easy to disband an army as some would think, and the Depot Brigades who handle this work are kept busy night and day. Replacements from every part of the country get assembled in one company, and when discharged, they must be in the zone nearest their homes; consequently the men have to be segregated by zones.

The men, who are from the zone in which the camp is located (*New York),* are discharged there. All others are shipped to a proper camp.

Every man's record has to be searched to see that he does not owe the government anything. Any mistakes in pay have to be rectified, before final payment is made. The men must attend three lectures, each consuming one-half day. These are to acquaint the men with problems that will confront them as soon as released, and also to help make a better country morally.

A physical examination consumes another half day. This is to determine the degree of one's disability, and is the basis for payments of any compensation. If anyone has an ailment curable, he is not discharged until cured; if permanently disabled in line of duty, he will receive a pension according to degree of disability. In any case, the soldier upon being discharged has to sign a statement which prevents him from over putting in claims other than those existing at date of discharge.

Application for employment is also made, if desired, and the soldier is referred to some company or individual as near his home as possible who wishes men in whatever particular line of work he states. All equipment has to be turned in, and one is kept busy from the beginning to the end of the process. The last morning, you are paid and then taken to the station, and, after you board the train and start, you are an ordinary civilian once more, but disguised in a soldier's uniform.

Parade Retards Demobilization

Tuesday, we were busy until late at night and Wednesday morning we were at it again, when all at once we were told to go back to our barracks, as orders had been received cancelling demobilization of the regiment.

Later in the day, we were informed that our Colonel, who was with another detachment of the regiment on another ship, had arrived, and upon hearing that we were being discharged, had telegraphed to G.H.Q. requesting permission to parade.

This we did the following Monday, and were the first intact fighting unit to march under the great Victory Arch, which was then in course of construction.

During a halt in the parade, one of the wounded heroes, who was riding in an automobile, threw up his helmet, and in an effort to get it, two men were killed.

We were also the first body of U.S. troops to parade in the French mass formation in America.

After a bountiful feast in the afternoon, we returned to camp, and again the wheels of demobilization began rolling.

In French phalanx formation – the pride of Harlem & NY City

Discharged From Service

Friday morning, February 22d, we passed the pay window and received our discharges and final pay. It was a year, seven months and seven days since we had been mobilized by order of the President; not so very long under ordinary circumstances, but when a larger part of it is spent on the battlefield, it seems ages. I could not help noticing a recruiting office on the opposite side of the road from where we were discharged, nor could I help noticing how far from it the men tried to get as they stood waiting for their turn.

As we marched to the station, we began to think of the new life we were soon to enter and how much different it would seem to us now with our broadened views and bitter knowledge of the world in general.

It seemed strange to think of having to provide for one's self, after being fed, clothed and housed by Uncle Sam's generous hand so long. With these thoughts and those of home, we boarded the train.

And when it finally started—Oh Boy! But I will leave the rest to the reader's imagination.

THE END.

Men of the regiment on arriving home.

PART TWO

"Somewhere in France"
Diary of C. J. Peterson since he started for France on
November 12, 1917

Nov. 12, 1917

We started the day by getting up at 3.15AM when the "first call" was sounded. The men knowing that we were to leave began preparing their packs. At 3.45 we had [reveille] after which the entire Battalion began [preparing to leave] the Armory.

At 6.00 we had roll call and final check up of the embarkation slips, we were also given two sandwiches apiece to eat for luncheon or at any time we choose. At 6.30 the Battalion swung out of the Armory and marched to the 166th St. "L" station and went to 96th St. where a ferry awaited them to take them across the river. I did not accompany them however, being detailed to assist in [packing] up equipment left by the A.W.O.L.'s etc. also to pick up stragglers who were wandering around and liable to come in at any moment. At 10.00AM my detail left taking a few prisoners who had come in. I do not mean that they were prisoners when they came in, but as soon as they arrived they were made such by Lieutenant Sidle [Seidel] who was officer of the guard and in charge of the detail. One or two however were brought in by detectives who were scouring the city trying to locate other deserters. We took the 3rd. Ave . "L" to ..... to Fulton St. and then took the tube to ..... assembled the regiment at..........

We quietly slipped out into the harbor and started our journey to France. As soon as we passed the Statue of Liberty I went to bed woke up sometime in the night by the tossing of the ship I knew that we were on our way.

Nov. 13, 1917

I got up at 5.30AM this morning and found that we were out of sight of land, it was a new sensation to us and I enjoyed it immensely.

At 10AM we could see by the sun that we were turning around and soon we were told that we were going back as something had happened to one of our engines and it would be impossible for us to keep up with the rest of the convoy. It seems to revive the spirits of many and everyone was in a conjovial mood. The band came up on deck and added to the merriment by playing for a couple of hours. At 8PM we sighted the lights of America.........

Nov. 14, 1917

Got up at 5.30AM and everyone came on deck to see where we were. But it was so foggy that it was impossible, but as the mist lifted we could distinguish Fort Hamilton and we knew that we were in New York. Hopes ran high as we all had hopes of going home for another last good-bye. One thing I wish to writing [write] now is the fact that you can hear [more] reports, [rumors,] stories etc. in this army than in any other place. And they keep one in a high pitch of excitement if you happen to pay any attention to them. After mess which is 7.30 we had an "abandon ship" drill. The band played and everyone was happy. We lay out in the harbor util 2.00PM when we came in here which was the same pier we left…

Nov. 15, 1917

As we lay here in dock to-day wondering what they were going to do with us a bugler relieved the monontony.........committing suicide.

But all they did was take us out on the pier and search us for ammunition, after which we were marched back on board the transport. I must confess that I was a little disappointed as I marched up the gangplank.

We were told however that we were to leave the ship the next morning. Once more everyone was in high spirits and the piano worked overtime that night, believe me.

Nov. 16, 1917

We got up this morning at 4.30 and after an early breakfast we began cleaning up the sleepoing compartments after which packs were made up and at 7.30 we "fell in" on the pier and we marched over to the station where we took the train to Dumont [NJ]. Then we got off and marched about one half mile to "Camp Merritt". This camp seemed to be a new one as they have only a few barracks built and work men are quite numerous. It is a busy place ... sunny rooms......

Nov. 17 to Dec. 2 both inclusive

There is not a great deal to record during this period. The weather was quite chilly, but most of our drilling with the excepttion of 3 or 4 days when we went on hikes, was done inside as every man in the Regiment had to qualify in the "course of musketry". I got two passes which then on one occasion I went to New York and borrowed some money (as I was broke) and went home on a Saturday and came back to Yorktown on Sunday eve, and returned to camp. Monday morning 23 hours late but nothing was said and I wish to say that it was my of ever [lasting luck that I avoided being punished for] staying overtime, but I realized that it might my last time and I could not resist the temptation. The following Saturday I got another pass and went to Yorktown was taken sick and returned Sunday evening. When I was away Serg't Schitia of Company J a Zulu who had seen service at the "front", shot and killed a fellow [Joseph Fagen, Co. I, on Nov. 25th] wounding a second in an argument over a game of dice. I had an attack of grip and was in bed most of the week.

We had an excellent dinner Thanksgiving, turkey and every-thing…with it then some sour rum….. Camp a few days prior to the departure of troops, we were not allowed to write anymore but I smuggled some mail out, whether the parties mailed them or not I do not know. The quarantine was raised Thanksgiving afternoon and a few visitors came and the boys enjoyed themselves with athletic games.

Dec. 3, 1917

This morning we got up at 5.30 and after mess prepared to leave and by 8.30 the camp was in practically the same condition as we found it. We took the train at Dumont and bid farewell to Camp Merritt, Tenafly, NJ going back to Hoboken where we boarded the same transport that we had once tried to cross the ocean on.

We had not been here long before we found out that a fire had been discovered in the coal in several of the bunkers and that it will have to be unloaded and coaled again which will take several days. In all probabilities we will go back to Tenafly as troops cannot be kept on a ship in port… The fact that 3 bombs were…and our present bad luck…as if this….

Dec. 4, to Dec. 11, both inclusive

Contrary to my belief we were not taken back to camp but remained on board doing very little except about an hour's exercise on the pier daily which was almost a necessity to get our limbs straightened out and to get a bit of fresh air.

No one can imagine how suffocating the hold of a ship is, especially when filled with troops until you have been compelled to stay there.

I was put on guard for this return trip and relieved from all other duties. I rather liked the idea as it will relieve the monotony somewhat. It was quite a job to unload the coal as it had to be done by hand with baskets holding perhaps 75 pounds. It took until Friday to get it all out as there was 3,200 tons. Loading was much easier as it was done by machinery and late Sunday eve., Dec. 11, 1917 we were all loaded and once more ready for our trip.

Dec. 12, 1917

This morning one of the firemen told us that we must be going to leave soon, as they had received orders to steam up. I soon found this to be true as the sailors began putting the …. watch-outs and in other ways making [preparations]…a tug came and…harbor where we…

I sat up quite late so as to have a last look at old New York but as we did not start I got tired bidding it farewell I went to bed.

Dec. 13, 1917

I got up this morning and found that we were in exactly the same place as when I went to bed. It started snowing this afternoon and as I write the wind is blowing and we are bound for France. I do not envy the sailors who have to go in the crow's nest or stand watch on the decks.

Dec. 14, 1917

I got up at 1.30AM as I have a relief that is on from 2.00 to 4.00 and as I went up on my posts which luckily were inside ones, I saw all the officers around, both ship and regimental. I asked one of the guards what the trouble was and he said that the storm had been so severe that the fleet put back to harbor and that we were struck by an oil freighter at about 12.00 o'clock after we and anchored…it was next to impossible [to sail,]…the damage [was so severe]…had to be abandon….

When daylight came I saw we were struck on the starboard bow about 20 or 25 ft. above the water line tearing a hole, big enough for two men to walk through side by side. If this ship isn't a "Voodoo" I am not in the army.

Immediately after mess they took some of the soldiers who assisted the sailors in tearing away the smashed steel plates and put a wooden patch over the hole. I am afraid that if we are torpedoed on this trip while I am asleep that I will be left as I never felt the shock last night. They put the lights out at 8.00 tonight and shortly after we weighed anchor and silently moved out of the harbor.

Dec.15, 1917
This morning when I got up we were traveling East "full steam ahead". We went up on deck this afternoon and had a little exercise. All we can see is sky and water with the exception of the ships in our convoy.

Dec. 16, 1917
Today we traveled at full speed with a smooth sea…
…a row boat. Lots of the fellows are sleeping fully dressed, afraid of being torpedoed. We had an "abandon ship" drill today. It takes us 11 1/2 minutes to get on B deck where I am supposed to take the whale boat from, I call that pretty good time from "Deck 3" and if everyone made as good time everyone could leave the ship in 20 minutes and it is hardly possible that it would go down in under 30 minutes if torpedoed.

No one is sea-sick yet.

Dec. 17, 1917

I went out on the well-deck this morning and as I was going through the door to go out when a huge wave came over soaking everyone who was out there, had I been a minute sooner I too, would have gotten a bath. I call the sea rough but the [the sailors] say not, though I think they are kidding us. Some of the boys are getting sea-sick and I expect near before long and believe me, I don't think much of it. Lights are lit at 7.10 A.M. and go [out at dusk] so our days are short as....

Tuesday, Dec. 18, 1917

Well! Well! Well! Talk about people being sea sick. I never saw so many in my life, and the expression on their faces would touch a heart of stone. Every muscle in their bodies relaxed and they do not seem to have strength enough [to] tighten them up. Although I am not sea-sick, the salty swell and the constant tossing of the ship are both very offensive.

The sea is very rough and I was watching some of the other ships their bows go out of sight in the water and then they come up until you can see the bottom of them. One almost forgets that it is winter and that when we left America it was covered with snow in the north, it is warm as summer owing to the fact that we are in the Gulf Stream.

Dec. 19, 1917

There was nothing of importance to record today. We passed an old freighter bound for New York, and also one yesterday. Of course each one was investigated by the cruiser which accompanied [us.] … they would be sighted the cruiser would rush ….. before the fleet would …….. full of soldiers.

When all at once a wave would sweep over and completely soak them, they would immediately leave and soon a new bunch would come out and get the same medicine. There are lots of sea-sick boys I am feeling better than I did, and if I was sea-sick which I will not admit it must have been very mild as I have not lost a meal or fed the fishes.

Dec. 20, 1917
I got up at 7.00 o'clock ….. and went up on deck …….. the sea air makes ………. acclimated. The …….
…in target practice. It is surprising to see how accurately and fast the guns can be fired. As soon as the first shot was fired the morning the soldiers packed the decks and they remained all day. Each night the boys have been going out on deck to sleep (a good many at least) but tonight a big wave struck "A" deck starboard soaking both men and blankets. It is needless to say that they left immediately. I have been getting some hot bread as I came off guard at 8.00 P.M. almost every night and you can bet that it is good.

Dec. 22, 1917
It rained a bit this morning but by 9 A.M. it was clear, it is strange how easily it can cloud up and rain and as quickly stop and clear off. For 3 days we have been drifting idly by day, going full speed at night they are still having target practice and I hear it rumored that we are holding back waiting for a French convoy. Our cruiser is still with us.

We continue [steaming east and we move] our watches every twenty minutes a head each [day]………. a lot of drifting.

Since we left the "States", as I suppose I will have to call home when I am over here on this side…

Dec. 23, 1917

This morning I saw the men on detail carrying barrels of turkeys towards the galley. With Christmas two days away it looks mighty suspicious. We had church this morning led by our Colonel who read two or three passages of scripture and said a few words, he offered a few suggestions which if carried out will have a tendency to make better soldiers of us. Major Dayton offered prayer and all in all I think if very helpful to all. Out here in the war zone amid the perils of the deep it is a great consiliation to know that there is some superior being who is watching over and protecting us. Today is our ninth day out and still no sight of land. We passed a neutral tramp this morning. I am rather enjoying myself now that all fear of seasickness is over.

Dec. 24, 1917

…. to my mind ………

to land. The men in the lower holds which means us too as I am on "Deck 3" were ordered to sleep on deck for the rest of the trip so as to be able to abandon ship quickly in case we are torpedoed. I guess we must be in the war zone.

Dec. 25, 1917

Merry Xmas and out of sight of land and in the war zone where any minute a submarine is liable to send a torpedo at us and send us to eternity via Davy Jones' locker. The French convoy which consists of 6 destroyers was picked up sometime during the night and the cruiser, which had been protecting us all the way over must have turned back during the night as I did not see it when I got up at daylight. I slept cold last night but I am not going to let that worry me as I will probably have a good many cold nights before this war is over

We had a turkey dinner today with all the trimmings but I found the turkey to be so tough that I could... I'll bet the pieces I had come...that was....

Dec. 26, 1917
Today is our twelfth day out and nothing has developed. No land. No submarines.

Dec. 27, 1917
9AM We sighted a lighthouse Hurrah! Hurrah! Hurrah! Although we are still fifty (50) miles from port you can bet that it is a most welcome sight to see something that is not floating but is on good old terra firma. I do not wonder now why Columbus kissed the ground when he discovered the New World. We passed the Greenwich meridian last night and watches were advanced 40 minutes, they tell us it is 5 ½ hours earlier than Eastern time but I have not bothered to figure it up. It does not get daylight until 8.00 now after the big jump in time last night. Two aero-planes came and met us about 25 miles out. To get our identity I imagine.

Dec. 28, 1917
I got up this morning not feeling very well, my jaws have sores...and when I came to eat...difficult job as I could....so I decided to [report to sick bay]...
[gap in text]
the glands of my neck. I could not find Corporal Curtis who answered sick call until after dinner. I then went up to the sick bay and the Doctor said he thought I may have mumps and to put me in the isolation ward which they did. I went to bed and had just got to sleep nicely when they woke me up and told me to get up as I was going ashore. I was put aboard an old scow with a lot of other sick fellows who were taken off the different ships in our convoy. When we reached the shore it was dark and raining a little. The first thing I

saw when I landed was four Ford ambulances that were waiting for the sick. We were taken at once to Naval Base Hospital #1 Not feeling very well I ate a little supper and went to bed.

Dec. 29, to Jan. 17 both inclusive

My time during this writing period was spent in the hospital where I was treated very nicely. The next day after I got in here I began to wonder what I would do for cigarettes etc. as I had no money but the following....first came in with mumps and I sent....he replied by sending......comfortable as...................sick some of the time though, in fact I was delirious 4 days. I became acquainted with 3 fellows who were at the front last fall and who were detailed down here on the Christmas mail detail. They told some great tales believe me, but I suppose I will see some of it myself in the near future. I cannot see out in the street from my ward and as I was closed up in the ambulance when I came here I have not as yet seen a bit of this place, but the Dr. said today that I could get out tomorrow and I certainly willing to go as I want to get back to my company where I know the boys, being amongst strange people in a strange land is not at all pleasant after a few days. Since I have been in here I must have met Serg't Her [not identified], who used to be with the regiment when it was at Peekskill, NY. He tells me that convoys are coming in two or three times a week.

Jan. 18, 1918

I got up this morning for the first time since...As soon as I had breakfast..........but it was 11.00 o'clock...

[gap in text]

...assembled. Then they called the roll and a fellow was placed in charge to march us to headquarters. I was sent from headquarters to the Strordon [name not identified] barracks to await further orders. I reported to the Strordon camp and was assigned to...temporary. I was told that I would have to stay here until they had communicated with my company commander and he sent for me in all probability will be at once if the company is permanently stationed. As soon as I saw where I had to stay, I began to hope that I would be sent for before the night as I did not fancy sleeping in the quarters I am to, it being the dirtiest place I have ever seen. But I guess I will not be sent for so I will go to bed but had I known that I was coming to this I don't think I would have been so anxious to get out of the hospital.

Jan. 19, 1918
Today has been one of misery for me. All I have done is to wander around waiting for headquarters until my transportation is ready, But as.....to wait here for a ....for a long.......one of.....the Strordon sergeants gave us 1 Franc 13 sou which about equivalent to 30 cents in American money. It came in very acceptable.

Jan. 20, 1918
I got up this morning quite disgusted with surroundings but at 1.30 was told to [report to] headquarters and found that I had about 10 minutes to catch the train in and as we had nearly a mile the fellow who took me double timed nearly all the way. When we got to the station we found we that we had about 3 minutes.

The fellow who had the ticket was called for two fares and my ration money was waiting for me so we boarded the train and we were off. As soon as the train started I condemned the railroads of France. The train made very good time considering the grades they have but the roadbeds are firmer. The joints in the rails are not broken and you can count each rail as the car passes over it, I ... the springs are more... that brings what all....until 5.15 when.... Left at 6.00 and at 10.00 P.M. we arrived at F..... where an American soldier told us we would have to wait until 6.25 A.M. for our next train and that we could stay in the station. As I was not feeling well I unrolled by pack and made a bed into which I was soundly sleeping.

Jan. 21, 1918

I was awakened this morning by a bunch of French soldiers rushing about the waiting room grabbing their packages and jumping up I woke up my partner and grabbing my pack and bedding I rushed for the door only to find out it was not my train as it was only 4.00 A.M. I went back to bed and about an hour later the same thing occurred. I then stayed up and rolled my pack went across the street and bought some coffee and bread. I had another hour's ride on the train and then a mile and a half walk... Group #1 Base 3 Section #1 Where found my regiment was camped. I had expected to find the .... But I was disappointed....they are trying ..... fit to.

....encounter the conditions that await us at the front. The buildings are about 65 x 20 and have around 85 fellows in bunks which are built in groups of four upper and lower. Dirt floors and leaky roofs. I found the regiment was doing stevedore work and many are sick from colds etc. One of my company, James Anderson had died from severe internal trouble. The Capt. told us to stay in for 3 or 4 days and rest up.

Jan. 22 to 29, both inclusive.

There is not much to record during this period. I stuck around the barracks helping the Co. clerk with some paper work. We were on guard once and I went out with them. I had a pass to go to the [St. N] [St. Nazaire] one afternoon, but the difficulty in making the people understand and the high high prices as well as the fact that that there is nothing American in the shops quite discouraged me. I do not think I will bother with town folks much. Believe me this is some life over here with the "overseas forces".

Jan. 30, 1918

I went out with the company this A.M. We left at 6.30 and were taken by trucks to the station where we go on a special work train and were taken to BLANK where we are helping build a switch yard. The ground is soft ………. level, is dead level, and very wet but it is easy to lay [so there] is no grading to be done. We quit [work and marched] to camp about 5.30. We ………… that it is over ………….

…went out and built railroads. They had a mule that nobody could ride and when they unhooked for dinner there were several who were thrown in the water before they could be convinced.

Jan. 31, 1918
We were out in the rain all day today. I find that the rain does not affect the movements or pulses [of] the army. The scenes are quite fascinating along the road to work and I plan to get a seat by the window so I can take in everything. As we received no money since the first of November and most of the boys are broke. They give out cigarettes every evening, the money coming out of the company fund.

Feb. 1, 1918 to 10, inclusive
Again another period with little to record, we went out on the job each day and it really surprised me to see how fast a gang of men can lay a railroad, we went on guard Friday the 8th. And off yesterday at 9.00 and half of the company were given passes to town in the A.M. the balance in the P.M. We left camp at 6.30 P.M. and went up on the job and unloaded sand all night until 5.00 A.M. We then waited until 6.00 for trucks to take us back to camp arriving at 7.00. After mess all went to bed as 48 hours without sleep has made the [men extremely fatigued.] I did not go on guard but was sleepy so slept until noon…bought a pr. of leggings…I needed badly.

(Side note: Was paid for November on the 7th. at night. Received 131 F. 50ct)

February 11, 1918

Went to [Montoir] and built railroad as usual. The sergeant in charge tells me that there is to be 285 miles of track in this yard. I don't believe we will lack for work.

February 12, 1918

Same old job and to make matters worse it has been a wet nasty day.

Feb. 13, 1918

We did not go to [Montoir] today but went to [St. N] and unloaded cars, built some railroad etc. The railroad is right on a sidewalk and in order to get the proper level it had to be cut down about a foot.

Feb. 14, 1918

Went out on a job this A.M. in the rain but it cleared before 9 A.M. Whenever we work there is always a lot of stands to buy things from at noon time.

Feb. 15, 1918

The company went out to work as usual but I did not go as I have been put in charge of quarters permanently. I have it .... barracks clean using the ......owning to colds etc. and .....had a pass and took a trip ....

Feb. 16, 1918

The company went out as usual and everything went on as usual. I went to town in the evening but came back so as to take check at 9.00 P.M.

Feb. 17, 1918

This morning the company went on guard but had no sooner posted the first relief then they were relieved by Co. G and word was passed to the 3rd. Batt. Company to prepare to leave. Everybody was wondering where we were going but at non-com's school the captain said that we were going to a place about 60 miles distant to do guard duty around an artillery camp.

Feb.18, 1918
We have not done much today, drilled some in the morning and in the P.M. quite a few went to town on passes and others took baths and cleaned up generally.
Feb. 19, 1918
This A.M. the company went on guard again as they were not going away and it was trip time. I am in charge of quarters and as it….. I am in every day and did not have to go out.

Feb. 20, 1918
………………to night.
Nearly all the company has gone out on night detail unloading sand. It is gently raining bids fair to be a disagreeable night.

Feb. 21, 1918
This A.M. the night detail slept and those were in all night went out. In the P.M. most of them were set to work washing clothes condemned and other wise that had accumulated on the supply Serg't's hands. We had a very constructive non-com's school lasting about two and one have hours, designating targets, etc. through the new style field glass.

Feb. 22, 1918
Today I had quite a busy day cleaning up as they looked for some Major General to inspect camp, but as he never came near our barracks I did not [feel] fully rewarded for my efforts, still I had the satisfaction of seeing the place spotlessly clean.

Feb. 23, 1918

The company went out as usual had to prepare for another inspection with the …..entirely different. I went to….examination of my ears….hearing well. Lately [I have been feeling] better and with the medicine I got to drop in them, I look for a big improvement. The doctor gave me a prescription and going next door I found a full equipped drug store with a competent pharmacist in charge. Some hospital and recovery is [still] needed ? either.

Feb. 24, 1918

Got up at 6.30 this (Sunday) A.M. Had inspection of equipment also venereal which is had every two weeks. We are going to leave here tomorrow for some place unbeknown to us. I heard Lieut. tell our serg't. to give the boys all they could eat tomorrow noon and to feed over on trips. We are to leave here at 12.30 and get to destination some time tomorrow night.

Feb. 26, 1918

Arrived here [Camp Coetquidan] today after a very tiresome trip of 60 miles. We left camp No. 1 at 12.30 and marched to train which left at 2.30 P.M. But such traveling, we have side-tracked every 10 minutes and sometime early in the night, being asleep I do not know exactly we were left until about 8 or 8.30 A.M. The mess serg't built a fire along the track and we had a very good breakfast of bread, beans, bacon and …. We arrived at destination at 10.00 and linked to each ………… are quite comfortably situated ….. all hands.

Feb. 27, 1918

Today the company has been drilling. I understand that we were to have charge of all guard and provost duty but word came in that our men had been replaced by white fellows. I being half crazy with ear ache all afternoon. Had an appointment with Dr. at 1.30 but he did not show up. Had venereal inspection, signs of moving.

Feb. 28, 1918

We were mustered this A.M. and later in the day heard that we are to leave camp within 48 hours. Do not know how true this may be. Temporary on guard.

Mar. 1, 1918

This P.M. the company went on a 12 mile hike. I was in charge of quarters so did not accompany them. Was I glad?

Mar. 2, 1918

This A.M. we fell in for reveille with mess kits and immediately after mess we went to work at ... Was by the side of German prisoners all day. Guess we will not get away in 48 hours.

Mar. 3, 1918

We went on guard this A.M. and I did not escape. I am .... to make a trip around ....quite hard and ....
Earache I do not think much of that trip as it takes nearly 2 hours.

Mar. 4, 1918

Came off guard this A.M. and we did not drill, only had inspection of quarters. Went to movies at YMCA for the first time since I have been in the army.

Mar. 5, 1918

Went out on detail this A.M. in a hard rain but it turned to snow about 9.00. I was taken with cramps and had to come in about 10.30. Received an Xmas box from Mother last night. There were 8 or 10 cookies in it and I can assure you they tasted great after going without cake of any kind for several months. Capt. Fish who has been A.W.L for a week and a half turned up today.

Mar. 6, 1918

Went on guard this A.M. Nothing else to report.

Mar. 7, 1918

Came off guard this A.M. and took a hike this P.M. We marched route-step for [about] 7 miles but the pace was so fast it was very tiring.

Mar. 8, 1918

Went .... to get out.............................. It was very good. I also got my pockets filled with potatoes that lay around the job on the ground and I cooked some tonight. Also good.

Mar. 9, 1918

Co. was not relieved until noon today as there was inspection and inventory of all property. We had a very busy day and I helped the Supply serg't until "taps" figuring [equipment] up.

Mar. 11, 1918

I did not go out with the company today as I had to help the Co. clerk on Service Records & Pay Rolls. I find we are to leave tomorrow for some other camp but do not [know] anything about was we are to do.

Mar. 12, 1918

This A.M. we fell with Barrack bags for reveille and after piling them in heaps we made up our pack, had mess at 8.30. Pay call was blown at 11.55 and we were paid for Dec. At 4.00 we left for the train. The YMCA served us coffee at the station and at 5.30 we departed.

Mar. 15, 1918

After a very tiresome [journey, we arrived at] the most beautiful country.... This A.M. marched to this [place.] We are billeted in [Remicourt.] [We will be training] for the trenches in 3 weeks by French instructors. We took a hike this P.M. to an adjoining village which is Reg'tal H'dq't's [at Noirlieu].

Mar. 16, 1918

Took a hike today and all the men are signed up and put in squads. Received 8 letters. Hurrah

Mar. 17, 1918

St. Patrick's Day and I am within 15 miles of front line trenches. We were instructed in the use and care of the French rifle with which we are to be equipped. Are all out of cigarettes and no place to buy any. Our French instructors are very nice. Saw one air fight also. Some place.

Mar. 18, 1918

Began intensive training today. Am good and tired tonight

Mar. 19, 1918

It has been a rainy day but I did not go out in the P.M. staying in to work up the C[o]. council book. Were instructed in the management of gas masks at N.C.O. school.

Mar. 20, 1918

Co. was issued our masks today and instructed how to use.

Mar. 21, 1918

…………….. air fight ……………

Mar. 22, 1918
Drilled as usual, nothing of importance. French guns arrived.

Mar. 23, 1918
Our French belts and packs came in today. Took a 20 [mile hike]....

Mar. 24, 1918
Was made Supply Sergeant today, do not know whether I like it or not.

Mar. 25, 1918
This A.M. we received orders to prepare to leave this P.M and I sure had my hands full, also issued steel helmets. Tonight we are in comfortable quarters at a place called Herpont.

Mar. 26, 1918
The company went out & drilled but I stayed in arranging supplies.

Mar. 27, 1918
This evening a bunch of boys began shooting up some cartridges they have found about camp and the Colonel must have gotten provoked as we were sent out on a hike at 9.00 P.M. and did not return [until] midnight, some hike!

Mar. 28, 1918
Company ....
were not considered. I do not think we will hear much shooting from now on.

March 31, 1918
Easter Sunday and nothing but .. and drills

Monday Apr. 1, 1918

Today the boys began training with live grenades & one fellow was fatally hurt [soldier not identified]. We have our automatic rifles & will soon be going up to the third line.

Apr. 2 to Apr. 11, 1918

During this period we had very intensive training and as civilian inhabitants had abandoned these towns there is nothing to tell except troops. We see lots of French soldiers going to the front.

Cigarettes and tobacco are very hard to get. Until 3 or 4 days ago when some American YMCA van came in you could get no tobacco or cigarettes. I know some fellows to pay as high as 5 Francs ($1.00) for 1 bag Bull Durham. I paid 2 Francs (40 cents) myself. Tomorrow we are on leave for some…..the front. Our batt. has already ……….trenches and relieve them…..

Apr. 12, 1918

………kilometers

…at least the Co. did   I rod[e] with the supplies.   We are now 5 kilometers from the first lines and air raids, air fights, and bombardments are frequent occurrences.

Apr. 13 to 16, 1918

The rumor is that we leave for the trenches tomorrow but I have not been notified yet. There are no regular formations as an enemy [plane] would soon see send a large body of men.

Apr. 17- Apr. 30, 1918 both inclusive.

We have been in the trenches for a 5 day tour and tomorrow we leave again for another tour but 20 days this time. 3 or our men wounded…where we ….but accidentally.

May 1st, 1918

On the first of May we came into this sector relieving the first Batt. And to my surprise I found it to be a woods and swamps [Bois d'Hauzy]. On the night of the sixth there was an awful lot of m[achine] g[un] and f[rom] us firing owning to a fellow seeing 3 Germans.

May … 1918

Today we moved to….and I am more than pleased to….the most……

END OF JOURNAL

Appendix One
Wartime Letters from Sgt. Peterson

"Putnam County Courier"
At Camp Dix
Army Life in the 15th Infantry
Corporal Peterson of Kent Cliffs Writes
of His Experience in the Army.

Kent Cliffs, Monday. – A friend of Clinton J. Peterson of this place, a corporal in Co. K, 15th Infantry, N.Y.N.G., somewhere in New Jersey, writes to a friend as follows:

"I am going to drop you a line to let you know we are no longer at Camp Whitman but in one of the Federal concentration camps which will be used for the *conscripted men*, but do not know what section of the country will send its men here. We left Camp Whitman Wednesday, a.m., at 7 o'clock but did not entrain until 8:45, left at 9, arrived at this place at 10 p.m., same day, the only towns of any importance we passed through were Poughkeepsie, Maybrook, Warwick, N.Y., Belvedere, Phillipsburg, Lambertville and Trenton, N.J. We stopped at Warwick and got several milk cans of hot coffee which had been ordered by telegraph at 1:30 o'clock and then proceeded, being served with salmon sandwiches and coffee on the train.

"Believe me, this is some camp here. When we arrived here it was dark and cloudy and we could not tell much about the place. They marched us out into a field and gave the command "take two pace intervals to the left." We were then ordered to lie down and make ourselves as comfortable as we could. Gee, I slept great in my sleeping bag after a very tiresome trip. Yesterday we pitched camp and as we have not been issued any cots we, or at least a lot of us, have made wooden cots. I also made a little stand and a floor in front of my cot and I am very comfortable. Our duty here is that of guarding camp, more in the nature of a fire guard and police. There are only two companies here now, New Jersey Guardsmen and they are going to leave. I don't know how soon they will begin to come in but I think they are coming alright as they have 8,000 men putting up barracks.

"That's all you can see as far as the eye can reach. Railroads run through the camp and there are loads of lumber, carloads I mean.

"I don't know the routine yet, expect to go on duty tonight. One man got killed yesterday a.m. but not of our outfit, but I'll bet they get it as we have a wild outfit who will not stop to say 'halt' three times.

"I expect to be home for primaries if I can get a furlough and if I do will tell you more than I can take time to write, but you will be down here I guess by and by and will have an opportunity of seeing some of these wonders. It is eight miles around camp and I was told this a.m. that we are to have fifty thousand men here come time in September.

"Gee, I would enjoy a strawberry soda right now.

"With the best regards to all who might wonder how I am getting on, will close."

Corp. Clinton J. Peterson

Camp Dix
Wrightstown, N.J.
September 2, 1917

Editor of the Courier:

Having read in your paper from time to time, letters from people who were living or passing through places of interest in different parts of the country and as they always seemed so full of interest, I thought that perhaps I might be able to write some things of interest in connection with army life, telling of the different places we are stationed at, providing we are moved often enough to keep my letters from getting monotonous. I did not know that I could write letters suitable for publication, but having seen one published in your paper, which I had written for a friend, and which I had no idea would be published, encouraged me to such an extent that I will attempt to write one to each week as long as they are acceptable and it is convenient for me to do so.

My letter published in your issue of August 24 gives you an idea of the immensity of the camp; I said that it was eight miles around it; I cannot vouch for the accuracy of this, but I do know that the guards who are on the outposts are taken out in large Peerless army trucks, of which there are quite a number here, having been brought up from the Mexican border about six weeks ago, to be used in hauling provisions and in hauling building material from the sidings to the building sites. The entire work here is in charge of a firm by the name of Irwin & Leighton, contractors from Philadelphia. They are working on a percentage and I guess Uncle Sam must do the paying as it would take quite a large bank account to handle the situation. They have a force of about 8,000 men at work and around 600 teams, the minimum wage here is $3 per day for common laborers. I have no idea what they pay the skilled men, but at the minimum rate it makes quite a weekly pay-roll.

Here are some figures which were published in last week's "Camp Dix News," a paper published weekly by

Irwin & Leighton for the men working here. It is given away, but I hear they are going to charge five cents a copy for it soon.

Material used in construction of camp:

Lumber of all kinds, 30,000,000 board feet.

Roof paper and tarred felt, 9,350,000 square feet.

Wall board, 2,500,000 square feet.

Wood sash, 51,000.

Wood doors, 8,000.

Locks, knobs, hinges, bolts, etc., 199,000.

Cement, 7.500 barrels.

Nails, 7,000 kegs.

Stove pipe, inside of building only, 22,000 linear feet.

Here are some figures giving an idea of the amount of food consumed in one day by the men working here:

Meat, 8,650 lbs.; Potatoes, 100 bu.; Clams, 2,000 lbs.; Coffee, 500 lbs.; Bread, 5,000 loaves; Fish, 2,400 lbs.; Eggs, 900; Milk, 2,000 qts.; Butter, 720 lbs. Ice 4 or 5 tons.

This is the average daily consumption for the week ending Aug. 25, and they claim that it would be more for last week. This food is served in the various cafeterias, one of which is located at each section, some of them have a seating capacity of 1,500 and so well equipped that this number can be fed in an hour.

They have a police force here which from what I have heard is much more efficient than lots of small cities have.

And say, the fire department would make Fire Chief Smith open his eyes, they have several large trucks and the firemen are always waiting for a call, of course this is not a Volunteer Fire Dept., and a shift is always on duty as a fire is the one thing as everything around here is so flammable and until the carpenters finish and the debris cleaned up there is a liability of a fire breaking out at any moment.

They also have a hospital here with several M.Ds., ambulances, etc., as in 8,000 men there are always a lot sick, and if an epidemic was to break out I guess it would be appreciated.

There will be a Military Camp Base Hospital here with accommodations for 1,500 men, not that they expect that many soldiers to be sick at one time but it is to be used for convalescent soldiers sent from the front.

They want to hire laborers and as they furnish lodging free and one can get meals for 15 or 25 cents, all depending upon whether you want a good meal or a better meal and as they are trying to get all the men to sign up to go to France to work on the cantonments there it looks as if the job might last for quite a while yet, and when it does finish, one can enlist and go right into the trenches as they would be right there.

One need not complain about the unsteadiness of the job as they work 24 hours every day Sunday included and you put in as many hours as you want to, all night long you can hear the incessant hammering on some of the posts I have been stationed at. With a couple of hundred men at work on our building there are always a lot of hammers falling at one time.

The Paramount Picture Company was here one day and they took pictures of them putting up one of the 200-man barracks, which are 43 x 100 ft. from start; before a single hole was dug for the posts upon which the buildings rest to the finish when every bit of debris was cleaned up and the American flag put at the top of it.

Lots of officers have been coming in the past week and a few troops, some from Georgia and other points I have not been able to find out much about them as I do not wander around much, but I will tell you more about soldiers in my next letter.

With best regards to all, I am,

Corp. Clinton J. Peterson

Camp Dix, Wrightstown, N.J
September 10, 1917

Editor of the Courier:

I am very sorry that I could not get this letter written yesterday so as to get it mailed today, but trust that it reach you in time for publication this week, but as I was N.C.O. (non-commissioned officer) in charge of quarters and it was my duty to see that the street was kept clean and then confine to quarters as punishment did not leave the street from "reveille" to "taps" and in addition to this I had a bunch of men who were on "fatigue" and I had to see that they kept busy so you can see that I was kept busy myself. We had just turned in for the night when Captain Fish came through the street and had all the men, excepting rookies, placed in tents near each other with orders to hold themselves in readiness for a hurry call as trouble was expected from some I.W.W.'s, in a nearby town and they expected to have to send men down. They sent a detachment to the place but nothing happened so we were not disturbed. But I had quite a feeling of security with all the fellows lying around fully dressed, rifles lying right by them ready to "fall in" at the first blast of the whistle.

It is beginning to get real chilly down here nights and I suppose it must be up there. We are being fed very good and with the hours of drill shortened the boys are having a very good time as they have only to go on guard every other night and at most of the posts they only have to do four hours duty during the night, and when they are on for twenty-four hours they only have to do eight hours as they are on two hours and off four.

The camp is being wired for electricity and already about half of it is illuminated by modern light. I presume our camp site is to be occupied by barracks as they had a trenching machine digging a ditch through one of the company streets today preparatory to laying sewer pipes. It was not a very large machine but I saw one the other day which was about fifteen feet wide by thirty feet long and the men who worked on it said that it would dig a trench thirty inches wide by eleven feet deep, 1,600 feet long in a ten hour day, but that is not based on such soil as you find in Carmel and Kent but in the sandy soil of New Jersey where you never see a stone as large as a hen's egg.

There has been two fires since we have been here but of consequence, we were "fell in: and marched up near them but were not needed as they were put out by hand extinguishers, but fires are not given any chance here; as soon as a fire is discovered every one is on the alert. I am expecting to hear the "fire call" sounded some night when every one is asleep to see how quickly we can assemble.

I will not have time to write much this time but will have a long letter next time, judging by the way the conscripts are coming in, I ought to find lots to write about. I have been promoted to sergeant since I wrote last and am very glad that I enlisted as soon as I did, because the chances for advancement were never so great as now.

I expect to come home Saturday and stay for two or three days while opportunity offers as no one knows how long we will be here.

Sgt. C. J. Peterson

Camp Dix
Wrightstown, N.J.
September 23, 1917

Editor of Courier:

Being on guard tonight and wanting to keep me awake will write you a letter telling you of some more of the wonderful things one sees here which may be interesting to some of your readers.

I think that my letter should be dated the 24th as it is now 12:45 a.m. and I suppose another day has started. Tonight I am stationed at the section which has the "observation tower" spoken of in a previous letter, upon which a man is posted to watch out for fires during the night while most of the camp is asleep, of course it is never all asleep as work is carried on in some of the sections night and day preparing for the new National Army which will soon be here in full strength. I do not know what per cent of it is here now but there is a large bunch of embryo soldiers here.

They have a telephone on top of this tower to be used in case of fire to summon the fire department, and at midnight each night the sergeant in charge of this section has to call up the commander of the guard at the guard house and report whether or not the cantonment is O.K. I have just been up there and reported before starting this letter and find that the weather up there is very cool and I am sure that the overcoats which were issued last evening will be appreciated by the men walking their posts. We are much better equipped than the men of the National Army as they have no clothing except those which they wore from home except for a few who have been issued uniforms; they have spring cots, a bed sack which when filled with straw makes a very good apology for a mattress and two blankets, in addition to this, our battalion has, for every man, a "poncho," a "shelter half" and an overcoat, so when one gets all this covering over him at night it is impossible to get cold. It was a very pleasant day today, not getting cold until evening, and to me it seemed as if everyone in New Jersey was here, as far as one could see was automobiles packed in the fields and lined up on either side of the roads and in the roads was one moving mass of machines. Most of the men here are from this state and the camp being within motoring distances I suppose the relatives came to see how the boys were getting along. When I mounted guard at 2:30 p.m., we went out on our parade ground and when the band, which by the way, is the only one here, started playing the crowd came up and kept closing up until it was almost impossible to get out when we finished and started to march away. I saw some crowds at Camp Whitman last year when visitors came to visit the 17,000 soldiers which were there at our time but they were almost insignificant by comparison.

Conscripts are coming in daily now and it would seem to be quite a difficult matter to take a lot of men, all green, and train them at one time, but the way it is arranged it is not so bad. When the first batch came in here they were split up 4 or 5 men being assigned to each company and when the next back came in they were distributed likewise and by that time the first batch were drilled enough to help drill the newer ones and as each lot comes in they are distributed through the different regiments so that only a few men are raw recruits at one time, one disadvantage to this from the conscripts standpoint is that you are not sure that 2 men from the same town will be in the same company even though they were all drafted at the same time, and again a whole bunch of fellows might be assigned to the same company. I have been talking with some of the fellows and I do not find many who are dissatisfied, as a whole, they seem willing to do their "bit."

Several new officers have been assigned to our battalion since we came here and hear that each Company is to have 2 Captains, 2 first and 2 second lieutenants according to the French idea, this is done so that one is shot there will be another to take his place.

Here is one of the "cheer up" songs which the boys are singing and which I think is so good every one ought to be singing it. It is sung to the tune of "Dixie."

LET'S GO
In khaki suit and army visor,
    All aboard to can the Kaiser,
Look away! Look away! Look away, Germany.
In Kaiserland he reigns alone;
    We'll push the Kaiser off his throne:
Look away! Look away! Look away, Germany.
We're off to can the Kaiser,
    Hooray! Hooray!
In Kaiserland we'll take our stand
    Until we can the Kaiser.
Let's go, let's go, let's go and can the Kaiser.

We have lots of others but this one strikes me as being the best.

I do not know of any place that offers the business opportunities that Wrightstown does. Already it has jumped from a small place with 2 or 3 stores, a hotel and depot to 12 or 15 stores, a lumber yard and several other enterprises I will not stop to enumerate. Of course 40,000 men will make quite a city and there will be undoubtedly be that number here as long as the war lasts with a new batch every 3 to 6 months and they have got to have some place to spend their money and there is something more than a mere living to the first to get in here and enter in the right line.

Hoping to be able to get another letter for next week, I am,

Respectfully yours,
Serg't C.J. Peterson

Sgt. Peterson is in Active Service

The following letter is from Sgt. Clinton Peterson, who is a member of Captain Fish's regiment in France, was received by Coleman S. Townsend recently.

August 7, 1918

Dear Friend Colie;

Received a letter from mother tonight and she said that you wanted to know why I had not written you, so before I answer hers, I will write you a few lines to sort of apologize for not writing sooner, but when I tell you that I have been very, very busy trying to help stop the great German offensive, I guess you will forgive me a little.

Believe me, Colie, I have seen some things long to be remembered; things that make one shudder in civilian life, and there is one thing that Capt. Fish and myself saw which I shall be most sure to tell you when I return. No, there is no danger of my forgetting it. If I were to live one hundred years, I know that it would be quite fresh in my memory; so even though the censor will not allow me to write it now, there is no danger of my forgetting it.

We are still with the French Army and do not see much of the American forces, except for an American Battery which is behind us; but from what I have heard and seen in the "Stars and Stripes," they are doing great work and as they have never yet met defeat, I have great hopes. But when one has been over here for a while, they sort of get over the idea of whipping the "Huns" in a week or two and going back home again. I remember when I was in the hospital in Brest, last January, I met some boys who had been at the front in October; and I was all fight at that time and told them that the war would be all over in a few months, but they laughed at me and told me that when I got to the front I would find out differently. I HAVE.

The conditions here are such that neither side can do much without a sacrifice that would be more than pay for anything that might be gained. Woodchucks live in tree tops as compared to the depths that we go in some of the dug-outs, and Fritz nor anyone else has anything that can make you go out, as far as shelling is concerned.

The weather has been quite pleasant for the past two or three months but I cannot recall anything as hot as some of the days we had last July when we were at Camp Whitman. I am told that winter starts in around October and already I am beginning to dread the thoughts of a winter in the trenches, and from all prospects I believe that it will find me there.

The package of "smokes" which you sent me never arrived, but it is not strange as a great many have been either lost or stolen: I can hardly find words to thank you for them, however, as it was no fault of yours that they never arrived.

Capt. Fish has been away for a couple of weeks so I cannot give you a very accurate account of his health, but as he was O.K. when he left and I have heard nothing to the contrary I presume that he must be alive at least. He is attending some sort of Infantry school, for, as you know, it is necessary to go to school at least once a year, if not twice; military tactics change so often and completely.

Some time when you are in Carmel, I wish you would drop in the Courier office and see what has happened to my paper. In the second week of June, I received six copies all at once and none since. I have written to mother to see about renewing my subscription which runs out in September and you cannot imagine how much I look forward to the coming of old Put. Co. news.

Well, Coleman, I have lots to do all the time and so cannot spend too much time but will drop you a letter at frequent intervals.

With best regards to all and that includes all your friends, of course, I beg to remain, as ever,

Your old Friend,
Sgt. Clinton J. Peterson
Company "K" – 369th R.I.U.S.
Secteur Postale 107 FRANCE

Appendix Two
Sgt. Peterson's Endorsement of Hamilton Fish, Jr.

"Newburgh Daily News" September 11, 1920
Letter of Endorsement for Hamilton Fish, Jr.

To the Editor of the News:

I am writing this letter in the hope you will give it space for the benefit of the people of Orange county and specially the colored ones. I would like everyone to know Major Hamilton Fish, jr., as I leaned to know him as a member of the National Guard and later on the battlefields of France. His executive ability, his leadership, his never-tiring efforts to secure everything possible for the comfort and betterment of those under him showed more than anything else could of his devotion. I shall never forget how, one evening in June, 1918, when the 369th U.S. Infantry Regiment (colored), formerly the 15th, was in the trenches on the edge of the Argonne we were given a gas attack by the enemy and Major Fish (then captain) was at the battalion headquarters in conference with other officers. As soon as word was received there of the attack, he, fearing for the safety of his men, donned his mask and going over-land, disregarding communication trenches, etc., never halted until he warned us of the attack. He received painful wounds from barbed wire.

On July 14 and 15, 1918, when the Germans made the last big attempt to take Paris, Major Fish's company was foremost of the regiment and was on the first line of the allied defense, where death seemed inevitable. I believe I knew his feelings as well as anyone, for I spent the night in the dugout with him as he waited for the barrage to lift and for the coming of the first wave of Germans and the opportunity to defend the flag of his country.

In September of the same year when we were in the midst of the Meuse-Argonne offensive and Major Fish was attending the staff school in Langres he obtained a leave of absence and while visiting points of interest along the front he heard that our regiment was engaged and he at once started to join us. About 30 percent of our organization had become casualties and it had practically ceased to act as a combat unit, there being no liaison between the various units. Our morale was about gone and the majority of our officers were either killed or wounded.

For 48 hours, under a most terrific rifle, machine gun and artillery fire, he traveled from company to company constantly exposed, reorganized us and made possible the attainment of our objective.

This is the type of candidate that I would like to see every colored voter support both at the primaries and on election day; one who will look after our best interests in peace as he did in war and who, to quote an oft-used phrase, is "tried and true."

Clinton J. Peterson
First Sgt., Co. K, 15 N.Y. Inf. (369th Regt.)
Kent Cliffs, Sept. 11

Appendix Three
Material Related to Captain Hamilton Fish, Jr.

"Poughkeepsie Eagle" April 18, 1917
Capt. Fish's Recruiting Drive

COLORED MEN OF THIS CITY
CAN ENLIST TO-DAY IN 15TH INF.

Eagle-News, Poughkeepsie, N. Y.
      Gentlemen:
     I shall be at 390 Main Street, Poughkeepsie at 12:30 P. M. on Wednesday, April 18th, to recruit colored men for the 15th Infantry National Guard stationed at New York. There are at present 1000 men enlisted and we expect to be mustered in by the Federal Government and sent into camp within the next two weeks.
     I would greatly appreciate it if you would give this some publicity as we want to recruit to 2000 men within the next thirty days, and I believe that there are a number of colored men in Poughkeepsie who would be glad to join.
     The 15th Infantry N. G. N. Y. was organized last July and accepted by the State in October. Col. William Hayward, Public Service Commissioner is Commanding Officer and Lorillard Spencer, the Governor's Military Secretary is Lieutenant Colonel.
     We were inspected a week ago Sunday by a Federal Army Officer who returned a favorable report, and the expectation is that we will be mustered in very shortly.
     I am going by automobile and will be in Beacon at 10:30 Wednesday, Wappinger Falls at 11:30, Poughkeepsie at 12:30 and will go to Newburgh at 3:30.
     As the time is very short this matter needs a good deal of publicity, and I hope you will do this for the sake of recruiting which I know you are strongly urging.
     Thanking you in advance,
              Very truly yours,
                 HAMILTON FISH, JR.,
            Captain 15th Infantry N. G. N. Y.

Fish telegram to Roosevelt, October 4, 1917

[To] Franklin Roosevelt
Navy Department Washington DC

Understand that a third battalion fifteenth New York Infantry colored is ordered to Spartanburg my brother officers believe with me that sending northern volunteer Negro troops south would cause recurrence if race troubles this battalion could render immediate valuable service in France on line of communications where there is great present need to relieve French troops why not solve difficult southern problem by letting these northern Negro soldiers go where they can be of immediate use and train for firing line quicker than in the south.
Captain Hamilton Fish, Jr.   10 a.m.

To father, October 23, 1917

Camp Wadsworth SC   Company "K"
Spartanburg   15TH Regiment N.Y. Infantry

Oct. 23/11

Dear Father,
I was directed not to write to anyone or telegraph the fact that we are to sail from Hoboken on Sat. Oct 27th so you must keep the news in strict confidence as it might have serious consequences if it leaked out. Personally, I think it is the kind of news that will be impossible to suppress but I do not want to be the one to give it out. The order reached us to-day from Washington and came like a bombshell and I must say all the officers are delighted. The situation between our soldiers and the poor whites of Spartanburg has been most critical since we arrived owning to the disgusting ------ [our] men received: Several serious race riots have just been prevented in the nick of time and all of us know that it was only a question of time before our men would retaliate and shoot up the town. The War Dept.

realizing the menacing situation ordered up to embark Sat. for Europe. Of course we are all glad to go and my only regret is not to see you and say goodbye…I want to ask you not to worry – the crossing is perfectly safe and we will not go to the firing line before March. I hope we will not be stuck in the line of communication but after four months training sent with the rest to the front. I honestly believe that I have the best company in the regt. and that they will follow me anywhere. I am quite proud of my company (K) which is not only the largest in numbers but has the best deport[ment]. Every regt. in the country will be envious of us when they hear the news. It is a privilege to fight for America and I am glad of the opportunity.

Fish to Father December 25, 1917

Today is Christmas Day and as I may not be with you I am taking advantage of a few hours…to write you, Tanta and Helena Merry Xmas.

Practically all our time is taken up with studying and taking military examinations. Lights are turned out at sundown which varies around 4:15 P.M. and not turned on again until about 7:30 A.M. This makes the day very short and the night horribly long.

Our routine consists of breakfast at eight o'clock, inspection of quarters at 10:30, lunch at twelve and examinations from 1:15 to 3:15, dinner at 3:30. In the morning we study our musketry bulletin for the afternoon exams which are always written and conducted just as in college under strict surveillance.

The nights are tedious and everlasting. There are no lights of any kind permitted and there are no diversions. Smoking is forbidden after sundown but of course that does not affect me. There have been no new developments and no one knows what we are going to do in France. It will take five months to place this regiment in the firing line and undoubtedly we will be sent to some big training camp in France…

We have seen no subs and I hope they are home for Xmas. If they come around they will have a warm reception.

With love to all

Affect., Hamilton

Hamilton Fish's Military Identification.

Letter from Fish to Franklin Roosevelt, January 1, 1918

WITH THE U.S. ARMED FORCES

Dear Franklin,

I am writing the following facts to you as a friend who has confidence in your discretion and as an American who believes in your good judgement and ability to remedy a condition which in the near future will endanger the lives of thousands of American soldiers and concerning the delay in disembarkation of troops in French ports which are under our control.

It was a great surprise to all of us to find that our convoy was not protected by destroyers until two days from the French coast. It now appears that our destroyers are protecting English grain ships to the detriment of the safety of American lives and ships. I have been reliably informed that American merchant ships have been obliged to enter port without any convoy owing to the above fact.

I have no desire to criticize anyone and only hope to remedy the condition before it results in a disaster especially as regards to transports.

The harbor facilities for handling disembarkation of troops and freight are utterly inadequate. Transports are compelled to wait weeks at a time to take their turn at disembarkation. The loss of time and the loss of use of the ships is of course very important but there is also the condition of the men to be considered which on account of the lack of space to exercise and the closeness of the quarters becomes worse every day spent on board ships. There have been epidemics of scarlet fever & mumps & pneumonia and the hospitals are crowded at the ports of disembarkation. I am told that there are twenty-five to thirty ships waiting to be unloaded at one port. We have been onboard our ship since Dec. 3 and there are ships in another harbor that are not as well off.

I write these facts from the standpoint of one not connected with the navy and therefore without any prejudice and trust you will understand the spirit in which this is sent for your personal consideration.
Sincerely yours,
Hamilton Fish, Jr.

Letter to father, January 13, 1918

Dear Father,

The mail system must be very inadequate as it is now six weeks since I have seen you and I have received no letters or news from home. I am looking forward to your letters and hope they will be delivered soon.

We are engaged at building a dam and constructing railroad for American use and will probably stay here until relieved by some newcomers. I imagine we will be here about a month and then will be sent to some training camp near the front. We have a considerable amount of freedom and lunch or dine in town three or four times a week. The food is excellent and cheap and the light wines or course delicious. I much prefer being here than in Tenafly where we were locked in. However I hope we will be sent nearer the front shortly to get in training. I cannot see how we could be sent into the trenches before June – so do not worry, as we have not received our machine guns yet and are lacking 1500 men.

I see no ending to this war for a long time on the basis of President Wilson's terms. In fact the Germans will be stronger than ever after they have signed a peace treaty with Russia so do not expect much from our army this year. Everyone here is talking about a great German offensive against France but I do not take any stock in it. Neither side is strong enough to break through and both realize the situation fully. Maybe the Central Powers will undertake an offensive in Italy if Russia is finally dispensed with.

I have been in charge of the Battalion as Major Spencer was left on the ship with measles which later developed into bronchitis, and he has not yet returned. I regret to inform you that dear old Major Dayton was transferred to the 1st Battalion while on board ship and we are not pleased with the exchange.

While on board ship, Col. Pickering gave the officers written exams which were strictly marked and an efficiency record kept of all the tests. I ranked second among the captains and had a much higher average than any of the majors. We had 12 exams of two hours duration each and we learned a great deal about musketry. I was fortunate to be detailed to go ashore the last day of the year to check up the baggage and owing to a squall was unable to return to the ship – with the consequence I had a most enjoyable New Year's Eve dinner and had the satisfaction of landing in France in 1917. I forgot to say we were held up a number of days on account of a lack of cars and had to stay on board ship until New Year's Day. We did not see any submarines but part of our convoy which left us a day from the French coast was attacked, and when we were near the French coast we received an SOS from a big ship about 20 miles away that had been hit.

Letter to father, January 23, 1918

…One of my men died suddenly in the barracks a few days ago and I went to the funeral yesterday. We took our band along and there were two other soldiers and one sailor buried at the same time. It was imposing as there were three different firing squads and the people along the road all stopped and took off their hats even the German prisoners as the autos with the bodies went by.

I have absolutely no war news or inside information. I hope to get up to the front sometime this summer but it will not be before July from the look of things now.

Letter to Sister, January 23, 1918

My company has been doing very good work and gave a splendid exhibition at guard mount yesterday. They have developed an excellent quartet which is in demand at all functions[;] Hospitals, Y.M.C.A. dinners, generals, etc. The K. Company quartet is as notorious as the band. I wish you could hear them.

Letter to father, February 19, 1918

....The French newspapers are filled with articles about the imminent German offensive, one would think that the attack was about to begin immediately but I feel confident that if there is to be any it will come long after you receive this letter. I believe the Germans will settle their Eastern affairs first before turning their attention to France. I hope that by July there may be some developments which will give an [indication] as to the duration of the war. The Col. still thinks that the war will be over by July 1st. I hope not as we want to get a chance to show our prowess.

We are anxiously awaiting orders to go to training camp.

Letter from Fish to father, April 8, 1918

Capt. Hamilton Fish, Jr.
369th U.S. Infantry, A.E.F.
Postal Secteur No. 54.

April 8, 1918

Dear Father:

I hope you will forgive me for not writing oftener but I am busy every moment getting my company ready for a tour of duty in the trenches. We expect to be ordered up in ten days and naturally there is a lot of polishing up to be done so that we can give a good account of ourselves on our introduction to the Boche. After all our wanderings and experiences, it is difficult to realize that we will be facing German bullets, and I hope taking German helmets before you get this letter. I understand helmets are the only things that we are allowed to keep, and also to send home.

Our regiment is the most envied American regiment in France and has the greatest opportunity to make a wonderful record. We are the only American regiment with the French Army and have the incomparable advantage of the instruction and experiences of the French. We are to all intents and purposes a part of the French Army and supplied by them with all of rifles, bayonets, helmets, gas masks, knapsacks, food and ammunition. The men look splendidly in the American khaki uniform and French leather equipment and brown helmets. I wonder what the Germans will think when they take one of our boys prisoner and find that he cannot speak French and comes from Harlem. I am a great believer in the fighting quality of the educated American Negro, provided he is well led. If the regiment does not make a splendid record, it will be the fault of the officers. I believe, if the censorship regulations were abolished, the 15th New York (now the 369th U.S. Infantry), would be so well known as the Rough Riders were in the Spanish-American War, before peace is declared. We were the second New York regiment over here, following closely on the old 69th, and I believe the first colored regiment to land in France. Today we are the American Foreign Legion of France. We are sending back our old 15th New York Infantry flag to Gov. Whitman to be placed with all the other old regimental flags in the State Capitol at Albany. It is quite appropriate that the flag should be returned to Gov. Whitman, as the regiment was organized during his administration and owes its success to his personal interest and efforts in its behalf.

We are billeted in a small village about fifteen miles from the front and are not bothered by German shells, but we can plainly hear the incessant rumble of the artillery. On clear nights the front looks like Fourth of July celebration with rockets, flares and flashes of big guns. Most of all the firing is now done at night time, because the artillery on both sides shell the lines of communication to prevent the bringing up of supplies and movement of troops. There are plenty of German aeroplanes hovering about, especially at night and there have been several air fights in the vicinity of our village. One of our battalions has already gone to the trenches. It was an interesting sight to see our troops march out of the little French village while our band played our National anthem, the Sombre and Meuse, the Marseilliaise.

There were no flowers or good-byes, as our boys marched out to give battle, but just the same, those of us who saw them go were greatly impressed by their martial appearance.

I have given up all attempts to figure on the duration of the war, as it is a waste of time. We know less about the German offensive than you do in America, as we do not get the German bulletins and the allied communiques are closely censored. From the latest reports the Germans have been checked in their attempt to take Amiens.

Please do not worry about my being hit, as it will not do either of us any good. There is no such thing as dodging a shell or a bullet, as the one that hits is never seen. It is a good deal a matter of luck, or, as the French say – "bonne chance." I am willing to take my chance with the rest of them.

We went through the throwing of hand grenades without accident, although one man dropped his and had the pluck to pick it up again and throw it out of the trench. Our boys already excel the French at grenade throwing on account of their baseball training. The hand grenade is one of the most important features of the present war, and has taken the place of the rifle to a large extent in trench warfare. Several of our men can throw dummy grenades seventy-five meters [246'], which is ten meters further than any of the French soldiers near here. Grenade throwing for distance, accuracy, and speed is the war sport of France, and has taken the place of football and other games.

H.R. is working in a French canteen less than twenty miles from here, and sent me a letter by one of our soldiers, who happened to pass by. I will try and go see here soon. Recently the town she was living in was severely bombed by German aviators. These air raids are always carried out on clear nights and we can distinctly hear the machines pass over our darkened little village on their mission of destruction. About a week ago, a French Officer told me that a single bomb had fallen there and killed forty-two non-combatants who had taken supposed shelter in the cellar of a house.

We declared war just one year ago and all reports indicate that America is aroused and enthusiastic for the prosecution of the war to victory. I am glad to hear that the nation has shaken off its shackles and destroyed the maggots of pacifism which feed on its carcass and lulled us into fancied security. I am confident that the farmers – the back-home folks, the plain people – whose sons in khaki, will bend every energy and make every sacrifice to bring this terrible war to a quick and successful conclusion.

Fish to father, May 1, 1918

Dear Father:

I have just come back from a tour of duty in the first line trenches and enjoyed our experience immensely. We were withdrawn before our ten days were up in order to move into another sector and we are now resting before taking up our new positions. The men lived up to my highest expectations and by their fearless conduct under heavy fire, showed that they have the willingness and ability to fight. My company lines were close to the German lines and in some places not more than fifty yards. The troops under my command were co-operating with an equal number of French troops, and were quartered with them. The condition and morale of my men were excellent and all wanted to remain in the first line trenches when the time for relief came. The food which was supplied and cooked by the French for our men was good and there was plenty of it. My men have never had better or more regular meals. The French captain with whom I quartered, received a menu of the mess daily and ordered any change he deemed necessary. The morale and spirit of the French soldier is wonderful and to a great degree due to their being supplied with regular and well prepared mess. The treatment of the men in the trenches by the French officers is one of comradeship and friendly supervision, especially the non-commissioned officers. The trenches are well constructed and kept in a good state of repair.

The organization of the French system of defense is based on the principal of increasing strength in depth. The first lines are lightly held and are merely outposts of surveillance. My platoons in the first lines were stationed in combat groups and very strongly protected on all sides by numerous rows of entanglements and by annamite (barbed wire) doors closing off both ends of the trench. One of my platoons was stationed in each combat group and at night were completely cut off. They had orders to resist to the last and with the enormous amount of wire entanglements which completely encircled these small strongholds, it would have been costly for the enemy to have attempted to capture any of them. Practically all the fighting is done at night or in the early morning. My men are contented, enjoy and show aptitude for night work, especially recon-noitering, and are delighted with the cordial treatment of both the French officers and soldiers.

I have just sent Governor Whitman a German helmet taken in a raid which my men co-operated with the French. The owner of the helmet was killed in action, but I regret to say that three Frenchmen were killed and three wounded, including a lieutenant, on the way back, by a German barrage. The storm of shells sounded exactly like a heavy gale at sea. The shriek of the shells was similar to the howling wind and the bursting of shells sounded like the crashing of big waves against the sides of the ship. The German barrage was pretty hot and accurate, while it lasted, and covered all our positions in a thick white cloud of powder smoke. One soon gets accustomed to the sound of the different shells and can easily recognize the departure from the arrivals, and the 75 from the 155. Of course, everyone sleeps in their clothes and do not take their shoes off for their tour in the trenches. There are innumerable rats and of all sizes, which eat up everything within smelling distance. They eat through the men's pockets and musette bags, climb over them at night and are generally a pest.

Letter to father, May 15, 1918

Capt Hamilton Fish
369th U.S. Inf. AEF
Secteur Postal 54

May 15, 1918

Dear Father,

I have just come back to the Reserve after having spent fifteen days in the front line trenches. It is quite a relief in many ways especially being able to get clean and to take ones shoes off at night. The men are in good spirits but very tired and dirty. I like the excitement of being in the front line trenches yet I am also glad to get a respite from the worries and responsibilities. To-day is the first real war & sunshining day we have had in the trenches. In fact it has been damp and cloudy ever since we came into this part of France two months ago.

Letter to father, May 19, 1918

May 19, 1918

Dear Father,

We moved back into Reserve a few days ago and are now constructing trenches & laying barbed wire about a mile from the German positions. We will stay here until we move back into our rest billet where all we have to do is to get clean eat and sleep.

Letter from Major Edwin Dayton to Captain Fish, May 24, 1918

FRANCE

May 24th, 1918.

My dear Captain Fish:

This month rounds out a full year of our mutual service in the 15th N.Y. Infantry, or as we are now called the 369th R.I.U.S. Our military paths seem about to diverge, and before that happens I want to tell you how thoroughly I appreciate the splendid and efficient support I had both from yourself and the fine company which you organized and commanded. In the many years of my long service I recall no company in any infantry regiment which was more efficiently and harmoniously built up to the personal standard of its commanding officer than I found your "K" company in the 3rd Battalion.

We were all justly proud of the good record of the battalion and I feel it only right to record my hearty appreciation of your sterling qualities as an officer and a man in many trying circumstances during the difficult period of organization.

Now we are both here for one purpose, to help with the war by doing our part in defeating the common enemy and if our paths run together again in the course of this undertaking it will be a great pleasure to renew our mutual service.

Yours sincerely,
Edwin W. Dayton
Major 369th R.I.U.S.

July 1918 from Fish's book – *Memoir of an American Patriot*
Capt. Fish believed this would be his last letter home.

Dear Father:

I have not received any mail from America for over two weeks, and I am afraid that the mail delivery has gone to pieces again. I am writing you a few lines to say that I am assigned with my company to two French companies to defend an important position (hill) against the expected German offensive. My company will be in the first position to resist the tremendous concentration against us and I do not believe there is any chance of us surviving the first push. I am proud to be trusted with such a post of honor and have the greatest confidence in my own men to do their duty to the end. The rest of our regiment is dug in far to the rear except for L and M companies; the latter is holding a village in our rear. My company is expected to protect the right flank of the position and to counterattack at sight of the first Boche. In war some units have to be sacrificed for the safety of the rest and this part has fallen to me and will be executed gladly as our contribution to final victory. How fond I am of you, and to thank you for all your care and devotion – words utterly fail me. I want you in case I am killed to be brave and remember that one could not wish a better way to die than for a righteous cause and one's country.

Love to Tanta, Grace, Rossy.

Your affectionate son,
Hamilton

Letter to Father July 18, 1918

Dear Father,

I think I wrote you that I went to Chalons in charge of the Band for the 4th of July and had a pleasant change. Harriet Rogers is doing splendid work in the Red Cross Canteen. I had to make several speeches in French and in spite of my vocabulary got away with the affair. On my return on July 5th we had an alert and had to occupy a new position at the front. The positions were disagreeable as we had to march three miles to there after dark and return before daylight. This meant we had to stay up all night for ten days waiting for the offensive which was a big [ ] because if the Boche attacked in force we would have all been lost as we were holding the front line. Fortunately for

221

my company the Boche did not attack but deluged us with all kinds of shells, killing three of my men, wounding five and gassing four badly. It was a terrible ordeal and the men stood it well. The shell fire was awful and I don't understand why our losses were not heavier. We all had narrow escapes. I had several being covered by dirt by a big shell in an open field and heavy shrapnel hit my helmet. Our positions were on the left flank of the offensive and in as much as the Boche did not attack we were shifted to the west to positions less than a mile from the front line and we are ready in case of a big attack. The shelling is pretty heavy here and goes on day and night so that it is difficult to bring up food supplies. I have not been able to write for the last two weeks as I have been exhausted and besides not getting a minute of sleep for over ten nights I have a touch of influenza which has now passed but have had a lot of extra work as two of my lieutenants are sick with the Spanish grippe and were evacuated a few days ago. I believe the Germans have received a very bad severe check all along the line but as usual you will probably hear more about the big battle than we do who are actually in it. I hope the Battle calms down soon as my company has been on the front for ninety days and it is exhausting besides I am due for a permission as soon as the offensive is beaten back. I need a change of scenery as it is almost five months that I have been at the front without a vacation except to Chalons on two occasions.

As I write there is a heavy bombardment going on overhead. We are gradually taking back our positions the ones given up for tactical reasons. My horse, a big powerful bay was killed yesterday in the stable by a shell much to my regret.

Letter to Virgina [last name not known], July 21, 1918

The last two weeks have been sleepless preparing and waiting for the German offensive. Consequently, when it broke loose we were ready for them and gave them a bad beating, which I hope will hasten the end of this fiendish war. My company was holding first line position on the night of the 15th, and if the Boche had attacked in force we would have all been sacrificed. It was not a pleasant anticipation to go through for ten successive nights, but luckily for us the Boche did not attack in force and contented themselves with smothering us with shells. My company lost three killed, six wounded and four badly gassed. The men conducted themselves bravely.

We are now acting as support for a French regiment in an active sector and the shells are constantly crashing overhead. I have had several narrow escapes, being hit by shrapnel on the helmet, and being covered by dirt from a big German shell in an open field. My horse, a fine, powerful bay, was killed a few days ago in a barn a couple of miles behind the lines. War is no respecter of men or animals. We have held the Boche all along the Champagne front in the intermediary positions and his losses have been very severe.

I hope to get my permission about the first of August or as soon as this battle has become stabilized. For the last five months I have been at or near the front and am ready for a change of environment.

Letter to father, October 10, 1918

Capt H Fish Jr
APO 714   Oct 10th 1918

Dear Father,
[Since] I last wrote...I have been through some exciting experiences since the close of the Line School on Sept. 26th and the beginning of the staff school on Oct. 5th... I am not permitted to write you about the fighting and can only say that the offensive in which our Regt took park surpassed my wildest imagination. Our losses especially among the officers were very heavy. Capt Cobb of White Plains who commanded the 2nd Ba was killed.   L.S.

[Lorillard Spencer] was wounded by machine gun fire but I do not know how badly I am very glad now that I joined the Regt and took part in the offensive. There is not much left of my company. McLoughlin came through without a scratch as did Sgt. Washington and Sgt. Peterson – the latter has just been made 1ˢᵗ Sgt of the company and has done excellent work. The Col. told me just as I was leaving that he would recommend me for a special decoration. I suppose a croix de guerre but there is a vast difference between recommendations and award. However, even a recommendation from such a source is extraordinary.

From Fish's book, *Memoir of an American Patriot*:

The Meuse-Argonne battle was the single most important battle of World War I. Had the German's succeeded, they would have had an open path into Paris and to the North Sea. But we stopped them. It was only a matter of time before Germany was compelled to surrender. At 11 A.M. on November 11, 1918, an armistice was declared, ending World War One. 'It seems almost a dream,' I wrote my father that day, 'in spite of the fact that peace had been discounted for the last two weeks. I am glad the killing of human beings is over and hope that it will be a lost art in the future.'

Nor will I forget the bravery of my loyal Sergeants, Clinton J. Peterson, Herman Brown, and William Layton, who carried out their duty to the men under heavy shelling at great risk to themselves. At the end of World War I, I told my men, 'You have fought and died for freedom and democracy. Now, you should go back home to the United States and continue to fight for your own freedom and democracy.'

"Putnam County Courier" January 31, 1919
Hamilton Fish, Jr. Cited
Honored by French for Giving Up Furlough to Join in Attack

New York, Tuesday – Captain Hamilton Fish, Jr., of Garrison, and Officer of the 369th Regiment (15th Regiment, New York State colored troops) has received the Croix de Guerre. The citation came from General Petain in the following words:

"Captain Hamilton Fish, Jr., commander of Company K of the 369th Infantry Regiment, being on furlough, came back to spend his furlough with the regiment, knowing it had been engaged. Has rendered precious services – exposed incessantly to danger – before, during, and after the taking of a village, and in establishing contact between the regiment and his battalion."

Captain Fish received the citation during the taking of the village of Sechault, in the Champagne, on Sept. 30. The Americans suffered heavy losses in the village – ten officers and several hundred men were killed.

Captain Fish was on a seven day's leave after graduating from the line school. His pass was good only for Paris, but he managed to get up to the front in time to join his regiment and take part in the big September offensive. He stayed with his organization until it was withdrawn, and then went to Paris. He then returned to the staff college and not been with his regiment since.

Captain Fish represented Putnam in the New York State Assembly for a number of years. He was a close friend and supporter of the late Colonel Roosevelt. He took an active part in recruiting the 15th Regiment of the New York State Guard, now the 369th Regiment. He is a son of Hamilton Fish of 810 Fifth Avenue, who was active in New York State politics for many years and who was Speaker of the New York State Legislature and is at present Chairman of the Republican County Committee of Putnam.

Captain Fish, at right, with General Hersey. Fish was an ambitious individual, but rather than stay in the safety of Paris during the Meuse-Argonne Offensive, he rushed to the front and heroically made his way to his men who were in the thick of combat.

Appendix Four
The Returning Hero

"Putnam County Courier" May 3, 1918
Kent Cliffs

Word has been received that Sgt. Clinton Peterson in France, has been made a second lieutenant and is expecting to be at the front of the battle line soon.

This appendix follows the post-war career of Sgt. Peterson. He was a local celebrity and local papers followed him for many years after the war, until he moved to New York City. After his first wife died unexpectedly, Peterson was at a temporary loss as to what to do. He remained rooted to Putnam County and became a well-respected community leader, both as a Boy Scout Troop leader and as a noted veteran.

The following items were published in the "Putnam County Courier."

February 7, 1919
Kent Cliffs Boy Member of Colored Infantry Honored by France.

Sgt. Clinton Peterson, of Kent Cliffs, has been award the Croix de Guerre medal by the French Government according to an announcement in the Sunday World containing a list received from Col. Hayward, the Commanding officer of the regiment.

Sgt. Peterson enlisted in the old 15th Infantry, N.Y.N.G., when it was being recruited and was a member of the company of which Hamilton Fish, Jr., was Captain. He has remained with Capt. Fish's company throughout the war and the regiment is now the 369th Infantry.

The world in its account says:

The heroic deeds of many of the other colored soldiers and their white officers have also been chronicled. Through all the tales runs the same thread of not only refusing to quit against odds but of fighting with redoubled fury against them, and of only being spurred to higher endeavors of courage and self-sacrifice by wounds.

It is expected that Sgt. Peterson will soon return to this country and his many friends are anxiously waiting to greet him.

February 10, 1919
Kent Cliffs

The many friends of Sgt. Clinton Peterson have received postal cards from him this week from Camp Upton at Yaphank, L.I. He returned from France with his regiment on Sunday and expects to be mustered out of the service next week and return to his home here.

February 14, 1919
Sgt. Peterson's Medal an Honor to Putnam
Editor Zickler Sends Congratulations from the South
to Hero's Aged Mother.

Pine Bluff, N.C. – I was indeed glad to read in the Courier that Sgt. Peterson was decorated by the French Government with the Croix de Guerre for bravery.

It is an honor to Kent, to Putnam County, and is most worthily bestowed.

There were more than 400,000 negroes in the United States army now being demobilized. Several of them, besides our sergeant, received the Distinguished Service Cross and the Croix de Guerre for extraordinary bravery and meritorious service. It is not strange that mass meetings are being planned in recognition of the patriotism and self-sacrifice of the negro soldiers, for these men had to meet a most insidious German propaganda, which extended not only through the industrial centers where negroes were gathered, but penetrated the very camps and cantonments where they were in training.

I want to congratulate his aged mother at Kent Cliffs. She must be very proud of her son just returned from France and who will probably join her at her home in Kent next week.

April 11, 1919
Church Honors Sgt. Peterson –
Presented Him with a Bible at Patriotic Service Which he Addressed.

Kent Cliffs, Thursday. The Baptist church at Kent Cliffs held a patriotic meeting on Tuesday evening. The program consisted of an opening selection, "America," prayer by Rev. A Christensen, of Troy, N.Y., a former pastor; solo "Long Long Trail," by Rev. A. Christensen, and a speech by Sergeant Clinton J. Peterson, during which he exhibited some relics of the world war and described the use of various articles that are part of the equipment of a solider in the United States Army. Sergeant Peterson then told some of the experiences of army life; camp, transportation, and the trenches, very vividly describing a scene of "no man's land" during an attack.

As an appreciation of what Sgt. Peterson had done in the great fight for world democracy, the members of the church presented him with a Bible. Rev. Willian Stocum, pastor of the church, made the presentation speech in which he spoke of the high efficiency of the American soldier, how we at home did our part through agriculture, buying stamps and bonds and giving to the various organizations that ministered to the welfare of our boys, both at home and abroad. He then very tenderly spoke of the good work of Sgt. Peterson as a soldier of Uncle Sam and exhorted him to be as good a soldier of Jesus Christ, and, as he had so carefully followed the instructions of his superior officers in the army, to likewise follow the instructions of the Great Maker, as set forth in the Book, as he was about to receive.

229

Sgt. Peterson, who is a member of the Kent Cliffs church, made a short response thanking the people for their kindness.

The services were brought to a close by the congregation singing the "Star Spangled Banner" and the benediction by the pastor.

The church was very beautifully decorated with the national colors and flags of the allied nations.

May 23, 1919

Sgt. Clinton Peterson has accepted the position of foreman on the farm of Hon. Hamilton Fish, Sr., at Garrison and he and his mother are now residing on the Fish estate there.

September 26, 1919
Sergeant Peterson Weds
Marriage to Miss Banks, of Yorktown, Took Place Sept. 17th.

Courier readers will be glad to extend heartiest congratulations to Sergeant Clinton Peterson and bride, Miss Maudenia Banks [Johnston]. The ceremony took place at the Presbyterian church of Yorktown, on Wednesday last, September 17, 1919.

The bride was most becomingly attired in white satin and carried white asters and maiden hair fern. She was attended by her niece, Miss Maudenia J. Williams, of Yorktown, who was attired in white silk voile and carried pink asters and maiden hair fern. The groom was attended by Sgt. Joseph Rantis, of Peekskill, also a member of the old 15th.

The ceremony was performed by the Rev. H.B. Roberts and Rev. W.J. Cumming, both of Yorktown. The bride was given away by her father.

The wedding march was played by Miss Edna Lee, of Yorktown, and "O Promise Me" was softly rendered during the ceremony. The church was very beautifully and appropriately decorated with flowers and flags.

Among the guests present were Mrs. Benson Array, Mrs. Alida Hutchinson, Mrs. Joseph Rantis, Mrs. Charles Hicks, Sr., and Mrs. Arthur Fauntleroy, of Peekskill; Mrs. Allie Williams, of New York, an aunt of the bride; George W. Johnston, of Amawalk, a brother of the bride; Miss Louise Peterson, of Baldwin Place, and also the entire congregation of the church which the bride was a member was represented.

The residents of Putnam County read Sgt. Peterson's very authentic account of his service overseas and the distinguished service which he rendered his country for which he received the Croix de Guerre and other decorations. Mr. and Mrs. Peterson will reside at Over-look Farm, the Fish estate, at Garrison.

Based on information from the 1920 census, Peterson was listed as age 28, black, living in Philipstown, Putnam County, occupation, farmer on a private estate. Married to Maudenia Peterson, age 29. Other members of the household include his mother, Nancy, age 60 [error], and a niece, Amanda E. Crawford, age 10.

"Highland Democrat" {Peekskill] October 10, 1920
Scouting Activities
Scoutmaster Peterson awards Boy Scout Troop Two of Peekskill

It was an honor night for Troop Two at the First Baptist Sunday School room Monday. Second Class badges had arrived for the boys who completed their tests in that rank at Camp Loyal and a good attendance was present to see them awarded. After a brief address of commendation and congratulation the Scoutmaster announced that the presentations would be made by one who knew what receiving the badge of honor meant for he had, himself, received the French Croix de Guerre, and introduced

Sergeant Clinton J. Peterson, Scoutmaster of Troop Seven. Mr. Peterson said that he did, indeed, appreciate the meaning of these badges for one of the inspirations that he and others of the American forces "over there" had felt was the knowledge that even the boys here in the United States were manfully doing their best to help a great cause. He addressed each boy as he presented his badge with words of congratulation and encouragement and when the ceremony was over receive in his turn an ovation of applause from the troop.

"Highland Democrat" October 20, 1920
Wife's Obituary

Mrs. Clinton J. Peterson

The many relatives and friends of Maudenia B. Johnston, wife of Clinton J. Peterson, of 115 South James street, Peekskill, were very much shocked by her sudden death, which occurred at 3.45 o'clock Saturday morning, Oct. 9, 1920. She was 29 years old, born in Yorktown Jan. 1, 1891, daughter of Mr. and Mrs. Daniel A. Johnston, and resided there until her marriage a little over a year ago.

She was a member of the Presbyterian Church of Yorktown and of its Christian Endeavor Society for many years.

The funeral services were held Monday afternoon at the above-named church and were and were conducted by Rev. H.B. Roberts, assisted by Rev. W.J. Cumming, both of Yorktown, the former of the church's present pastor and the latter retired. The esteem in which she was held was shown by the numerous beautiful floral tributes.

Mrs. Peterson leaves to mourn her loss besides her grief-stricken husband, her father and mother, a brother George W., a niece, Maudenia J. Williams, two aunts and an uncle.

Interment was made in the family plot at Yorktown.

The sympathy of the entire community goes out to the bereaved ones at this time.

Within a week of his wife's sudden death, Peterson sought the help of his former company commander, Hamilton Fish. The latter agreed to pay for Peterson to travel to the Caribbean on a business trip related to the cotton industry. Peterson applied for a passport and Fish provided the necessary affidavit and other information for it to be approved. Although Peterson did not go on this trip, it does illustrate his sense of loss and attempt at some type of diversion.

FORM OF AFFIDAVIT FOR OTHER THAN RELATIVE

Personally appeared before me, a Notary Public, one Hamilton Fatly _____ who on oath says:

That he has known Charles J. Peteru _____ who is an applicant for an American passport, for the past ___ years, and that to the best of his _____ knowledge and belief, the said Chas. J. Peteru _____ was born in the town of Kent on or about 7th day of June 1891.

The affiant bases his knowledge and belief upon the following facts:

_____ Charles J. Peteru served under my command A.K. 367 Inf. for two years. He was born in Petened Ky. _____ where I was born. I know his family well. His father is still _____

[signature] Hamilton Fatly
115 Broadway, New York

Subscribed and sworn to before me

this 14 day of October 19 29

[SEAL.]

_____ Notary Public.

Paragraph 6 of the "Rules governing the granting and issuing of passports in the United States," promulgated by the Department of State January 21, 1915, reads: ...

DESCRIPTION OF APPLICANT.

Age 29 years.   Mouth: Res ___
Stature 6 ft 0 in. Eng.   Chin: Round
Forehead: Broad   Hair: Black
Eyes: Brown   Complexion: Black
Nose: Medium   Face: Oblong
Distinguishing marks:

AFFIDAVIT OF IDENTIFYING WITNESS.

I, Hamilton Fatly Jr. _____ solemnly swear that I am a [native] [citizen] of the United States, that I reside at Bronx, New York, that I have known the above named Chas. J. Peteru personally for life, and that he is a native citizen of the United States, and that the facts stated in [my] affidavit are true to the best of my knowledge and belief.

[signature] Hamilton Fatly
115 Broadway, New York

Sworn to before me this ___ day of OCT 14 19___, at ___

[seal] Huldy H. Chen, _____

Applicant desires passport to be sent to the following address:

Hamilton Fatly
115 Broadway, New York

Hotel State
Washington D.C.
Oct 19 1930

Charles J. Peteru of Kent Pat Co Ky is going to the West Indies to engage in the cotton business in which I am interested.

Hamilton Fatly
Jamaica Pat Co Ky

One of the ways that we know that Peterson did not actually depart for the Caribbean is the following article from the local newspaper:

"Highland Democrat" November 6, 1920
Scouting news

The first Scoutmaster's round-table of the Ninth Westchester district was, so far as action was concerned, practically a district committee meeting, with the commissioned Scout officers present. Of the latter those in attendance were ...Scoutmaster Clinton J. Peterson, of Troop Seven, of Peekskill...Following this there was considerable informal talk of plans and methods and the meeting closed with a strong feeling of unison for revived and enlarged Scout work in the Ninth District.

"Highland Democrat" January 5, 1921

Candidates in Troop Three are required to pledge themselves to advance through the ranks of the organization with reasonable rapidity and members already in are spurred on to keep ahead of the new-comers, consequently [advance] the regular order of the troop. At the weekly meeting of the troop at Knights of Columbus Hall on Tuesday evening, one Scout completed his qualifications for Second Class and three others, previously qualified, were awarded their badges. Sergeant Clinton J. Peterson, Scoutmaster of Troop Seven, presented the badges with a short and appropriate address...Two hikes were announced for next Sunday (tomorrow); one, for patrol leaders and assistants, under the Scoutmaster, and one for the Cat, Fox and Cub Patrols, under the Senior Patrol Leader. The Scout game of "Compass" formed the recreation for the evening.

In 1921, Peterson was awarded the New York State Conspicuous Cross for his heroism in the war. Although no articles or other sources recount his acceptance of the medal, it is recorded as #1026 in the record of recipients. Dr. Jeffrey Sammons believes that the close friendship with Hamilton Fish, Peterson's former Company commander, played a role in the issuance of this medal. Its receipt just months after the unexpected death of his young wife certainly would have boosted his spirits.

"Highland Democrat" March 5, 1921
American Legion Officers

On Friday night of last week at S.O.V. hall, Peekskill Post No. 274, American Legion held a regular meeting. These officers were elected for the ensuing year: Walter Hooley, president; George McCann, Martin Weias, Joseph Rantis, vice presidents; Clinton Peterson, adjutant; Elbert H. Bagley, treasurer. The Executive Committee compromises Arthur C. Lee, chairman, Thomas Dain, Lester B. Lane, Edward M. Higgins, James Manning, Patrick J. Clarkin and John Knapp. A committee of six with George McCann, as chairman, will hold a dance on April 6.

On July 10, 1923, at the age of thirty-two, Peterson enlisted in the 369th Infantry, New York National Guard, which consisted of both many veterans of the old command, along with other World War veterans and men who did not see combat overseas. In regards to his civilian life, in the early 1920s, Peterson began his career with the postal service as described in the following article.

"Putnam County Courier" April 18, 1924
Lieut. Clinton J. Peterson in Mail Service
Former Resident of Kent Cliffs Recently Commissioned in New York National Guard

Clinton J. Peterson, of Yorktown, formerly of Kent, has been commissioned a second lieutenant of the New York National Guard. Of him the Peekskill Democrat has to say in its last issue:

"Lieut. Peterson is a World War veteran, having served with distinction with the 369th Infantry in France as a sergeant. After his return he wrote a series of articles concerning his experiences which were published in the Putnam County Courier and aroused wide and favorable comment. He took the examination for rural mail carrier at Peekskill, and passing with the highest average of those who were examined, was appointed to the rural free delivery route at Yorktown Heights. Later he took the examination for railway mail clerk, and secured an appointment, which position he now holds.

"Lieut. Peterson has many friends in Peekskill, who are much interested in his progress, not only because of his fine war record, but because of his ambition, ability and fine spirit. He is a member of Peekskill Post, No. 274, of the American Legion.

"Putnam County Republican" April 20, 1924
Military Honor for Clinton J. Peterson
Commissioned Second Lieutenant in New York National Guard

Clinton J. Peterson, who served in France in the World War, where he was a Sergeant with the 369th Infantry, has been honored by receiving a commission as a Second Lieutenant in the New York National Guard.

Lieutenant Peterson was born in Carmel and is well known in this section, where his boyhood days were spent. He made a good record over seas and some time after his return from the war he took the examination for R.F.D. carrier from Yorktown Heights, was successful, received the appointment and served satisfactorily for a number of years. Being ambitious and desirous of advancement, he took the examination of railway mail clerk, passed a good examination, and received appointment and is now filling that position. He is a painstaking, capable young man and always faithful to any trust committed to his care. His friends are pleased to learn of the honor bestowed on him and tender congratulations.

We are indebted to the courtesy of Mr. George E. Briggs, Editor of the "Highland Democrat," Peekskill, for the loan of the portrait cut of Mr. Peterson.

The news of Sergeant Peterson's promotion was also featured in the leading African-American newspaper of the time, the New York Age. From this date forward, the steady rise of Lieutenant Peterson to Major Peterson was reflected in numerous articles from the Age, and even other African-American papers in other parts of the country, including the Pittsburgh Courier and Washington D.C. Evening Star.

"New York Age" December 4, 1924
369th Infantry Non-Coms Win Shoulder Straps; Mikell Made 1st Lieut.

A group of seven non-commissioned officers of the 369th Infantry, N.Y.N.G., have won advancement to the ranks of commissioned officers. The following sergeants have been made second lieutenants and assigned to the duties indicated:

Staff Sergeant James W. Jones, to Co. I; 1st Sergeant Joseph McD. Smith to Co. L; Staff Sergeant Albert R. Clarkson to Co. H; 1st Sergeant Jose V. Gomez, to Co. C; Staff Sergeant Clinton J. Peterson to Co. A; 1st Sergeant Jack Coleman to Co. M; Sergeant Jacob Porter to be warrant office and band leader.

In addition to these, another honor was handed Second Lieutenant Eugene Mikell, who has been serving as band director. He has been promoted to a first lieutenancy and made conductor of Music.

The Boys' Cadet Band, under Lieut. Mikell, took part in the exercises in connection with the unveiling of the memorial tablets at the Plaza, 59th street and Fifth avenue, on Wednesday afternoon, April 9, marking the anniversary of the Appomattox surrender.

NY National Guard ID -1927.   EFHS

The state census for 1925 year showed Peterson living with the parents of his deceased wife at their home in Yorktown, Westchester County. Although his occupation was not listed in the state census, we know that Peterson was a rural route mail carrier. Others in the household included Maudenia Williams, niece of the Johnstons, their son, George Johnston, and Amanda Crawford, listed as a lodger.

"Highland Democrat" March 7, 1925
Sgt. Peterson reorganizes local Boy Scout Troop

Three or four years ago Peekskill had a small, but enthusiastic troop of colored Boy Scouts, with an exceptionally capable Scoutmaster. This was old Troop Seven, under Scoutmaster Clinton J. Peterson. As, unfortunately, often happens, the Scoutmaster moved and, unable to replace him, the team disbanded. Repeated efforts have been made to reorganize it but without success until Mr. Peterson returned to Peekskill. Now re-organized [the Troop] is well under way. Nearly twice as many boys as were in the old troop are enthused, an Assistant Scoutmaster has been secured, formative meetings have been held and a new charter for the revised troop is expected in the near future. They made their first appearance in a Scout gathering at the rally held last Saturday night.

Peterson was promoted to Captain of Company C, 369th in 1927. He is pictured here at Camp Smith, 1929. Courtesy of East Fishkill HS

In December 1929, Peterson married a second time. His new wife was Olga Graham, born in Louisiana about 1900 and like her new husband, she was a postal clerk with the railroad. Raised in Minnesota, Olga was a high school graduate and very lively. Photos of her while living in Harlem beginning in 1918 show a young woman filled with life and enjoying the Roaring Twenties. After their marriage, perhaps as their honeymoon, the two traveled to France and returned to New York in June, 1930.

"On the Roof in Lil' Ole' NY 1922. Olga at left.   EFHS

"New York Amsterdam News" December 4, 1929

MARRIAGE ANNOUNCED

—— Mrs. Clinton J. Peterson ——

Mr. and Mrs. Edward Graham have announced the marriage of their daughter, Olga, to Captain Clinton J. Peterson, at Greenwich Conn., on August 3.

Mrs. Peterson is director of the Children's Theatre at the West 131th street branch of the Y. W. C. A.

Mr. Peterson, a World War veteran, is a railway postal clerk. He served with the Old Fifteenth ("Hell Fighters") and was decorated by the French government for bravery in action and was awarded the Conspicuous Service Medal by the Legislature of New York State upon his return in 1919. At present he commands Company "C' of the 369th Infantry, N. Y. N. G.

The couple will be at home at 401 Edgecombe avenue, Apartment 6-D, after December 10.

241

The newlyweds lived in a brand-new apartment building in the Sugar Hill neighborhood of upper Manhattan at 401 Edgecomb Avenue. These were the Dunbar Apartments, built in 1927 exclusively for African Americans. Many famous people lived there, including W.E.B. DuBois and Bill "Bojangles" Robinson; in fact, it was nick-named the Celebrity House.

In the 1930 census, Peterson's age was mistakenly recorded as thirty-five (should have been thirty-nine) and Olga was thirty. Her mother, Anna Graham, aged fifty-eight, lived with them, but her father still resided in Minnesota. They paid eighty-five dollars a month in rent and had a radio. In addition to celebrity tenants, many residents in the building were originally from the south, with a sprinkling of West Indian neighbors and even a head of a family of three born in Africa. It was a melting pot of folks from different cultures and regions both within, and without, the United States, reflective of Harlem's reputation as a Mecca for blacks from around the world.

Captain Peterson's military career in the National Guard took him to training sites in Virginia, Georgia, and the annual exercises at Camp Smith, where he had joined the old 15th regiment in May 1917 (located at Peekskill, New York). There must have been a warming and comforting sense of continuity among the old comrades in the face of economic turmoil caused by the Great Depression. Ever the community man, Captain Peterson did what he could to help the less fortunate. The following two articles illustrate is stature as a well-respected military officer and his humanitarian sensibilities:

"Washington, D.C. Evening Star" May 24, 1931
25,000 Expected at Cadet Contest
Rival Colored High Schools to Compete on
Thursday Before Big Crowd

To climax the company competition, which will start at 9 o'clock and winds up at 4;30 o'clock, there will be a silent exhibition drill, a brigade review before Maj. Gen. Van Horn Mosely, deputy chief of staff, and at 5:30 p.m., the presentation of prizes.

The drills have been annually since 1893.

The judges will be Capt. Clinton J. Peterson, New York National Guard; Lieut. Thomas H. Chatmon, Maryland National Guard; Lieut. Sylvester Blackwell, Washington, and Lieut. Harry E. Dorsey (alternate), Maryland National Guard.

"New York Age" December 5, 1931
Harlem Accredited with Raising $65,000
to Date for Unemployment Relief

At a dinner for leaders and workers of the Harlem block-to-block canvas of the Emergency Unemployment Relief Committee given Wednesday, November 26, at the Little Grey Shop in West 145th street, Dr. John C. Curran, executive secretary of the Harlem Division, reported that to date $65,000 had been collected and accredited to Harlem.

The Hon. Grover A. Whalen, former Police Commissioner, was the principal speaker. Talks were made by the Hon. Fred R. Moore, Dr. Louis T. Wright, Miss Eva Parks, Mrs. Rosa L. Blocker and Capt. Clinton J. Peterson. Elmer A. Carter was chairman.

NYC Parade, 1932. Peterson on the right. EFHS

What greater expression of a person's professional standing in the United States military can there be other than as a part of the Guard of Honor for a newly-elected president? The following article is from the Pittsburgh Courier, an African American publication. From its description of the Inauguration of the Thirty-Second President of the United States, Franklin Delano Roosevelt, you easily catch the thrill of the day and the anticipation that a new chapter in American society for African Americans was at hand.

"Pittsburgh Courier" March 11, 1933
Describing President Roosevelt's Inaugural & Parade

Symbolic of the hope that rose in the heart of man, a shaft of bright sunshine fell at the Capitol steps as if wanting to disperse the clouds of economic difficulties which, a brief moment before, the new Executive had staunchily avowed to undo.

One by one, the unit making up the three-hour long parade filed past the reviewing stand. And as it passed his reviewing stand, it also passed by the hungry eyes of 500,000 men, women and children who saw the representative Negro at his best.

They saw, too, for the first time in this nation's history, a colored youth in the vanguard of the Presidential Guard of Honor, which is symbolic of the perpetuity of the government by all the people.

The saw, too, complete companies of colored Boy Scouts line up and protecting the line of march.

They saw, too, while the throngs applauded and roared itself hoarse, units of our own military, the Elks, the American Legion and college and High School Cadets marching in the parade with the neatness and precision of seasoned brigadiers.

They saw part of the "new deal" when Major General McArthur, mounted on a spirited charger, led the first parade unit which included the all-colored Machine Gun Company of the Tenth Cavalry, who mounted in natty khaki trappings, sabres drawn like the "long knives" of the Indian War, rode in perfect alignment with their comrades of more tumultuous times.

Mad enthusiasm, from both white and colored, greeted this unique detachment made up of members of the race. And as a prominent white woman near the writer remarked, "they deserve the plaudits of the world."

In the first division of the parade also marched the future leaders of the race. The R.O.T.C. battalion and band from Howard University failed to reveal a single misalignment in their close ranks. With military mien and precision, chins thrust forward, eyes in the alert to catch the slightest sign of a command, they strode in favorable contrast with the battle scarred veterans of the "War to End War."

The First Battalion of the 372nd Infantry, led by dashing Captain Arthur C. Newman, veteran of many wars, was the recipient of cheers that thundered well after his outfit was out of sight, together with other colored units in the first division of the parade. Ahead of three major divisions were still more representatives of the race. There was the Ninth Brigade Band, headed by Colonel Kelsey A. Pharr, high school Cadets from Armstrong, Dunbar and Cardozo; the R.O.T.C. from Howard University, in their smart blue and gold uniforms.

When these colored contingents passed the Court of Honor, President Roosevelt gave them a snappy salute of recognition which brought thunderous applause from the dignitaries seated on the Presidential flanks, and from those across the street from the reviewing stand.

And there was the American Legion marking to the martial tune of their own bands, and carried all the way down the avenue in a rising crescendo of vivas and applause.

The American Legion units represented were the James Reese Europe and the James Walker Posts together with their respective Women's Auxiliary units. All were under the command of George Hunt and George Stewart.

Among those who made up the Presidential Guard of honor were the following colored military officers: Captain Wilmer F. Lucas and Captain Clinton J. Peterson, both of the 369th Infantry; First Lieutenant Richard R. Queen, New Jersey National Guard; Captain William Creigler, Maryland National Guard and Lieutenants Gray and Chapman, both of the Maryland National Guard.

The parade was attended by the largest crowd ever massed at any one time within the limited confines of the District of Columbia…No less than 50,000 colored people from nearby states and from states as far as California were on hand to witness the festivities. Special delegations came from Chicago, Cleveland, Toledo, Philadelphia, Pittsburgh, and New York, swelled the ranks.

"New York Amsterdam News" January 10, 1934

Moves Up a Step

CAPTAIN GIVEN MAJOR'S RANK

Peterson Third Negro to Head Battalion of the 369th

A public promise made by its retired commander, Col. William A. Taylor, that the three field battalions of Harlem's 369th Infantry, New York National Guard, were to be placed under the command of Negro majors "by or about the first of the year" was fulfilled on Friday.

Capt. Clinton J. Peterson, formerly in command of Company "C" of the First Battalion, was promoted to major in an order under the date of January 5 from the offices of the adjutant general of the state.

Major Peterson will assume command of the Third Battalion, joining Majors Chauncey M. Cooper and Wilmer F. Lucas, who command, respectively, the First and Second Battalions. Enjoying a similar ranking in the regiment is Major Leo Pitz Nearon, who is attached to the staff of Col. John G. Grimley. Dr. Nearon is one of the officers eligible for the vacant post of lieutenant-colonel.

Major Peterson is a veteran of the World War, having served in France with the Old Fifteenth Regiment. He has been attached to the 369th Infantry for nine years. He is in the postal service and resides with his family at 2588 Eighth avenue.

Legion Post To Honor Taylor.

The Col. Charles Young Post of the American Legion will pay tribute to Col. William A. Taylor, who retired recently as commander of the 369th Regiment, with a banquet January 31 at the 137th street Y. C. A., Capt. M. V. Boutte announced yesterday.

Capt. Boutte said that a citizens' committee would co-operate with the post in giving the testimonial. He announced as members of the committee Dr. Leo Pitz Nearon, Mrs. Cecilia Cabaniss Saunders, Mrs. Sadie Warren Davis, Mrs. Ruth Logan Roberts, Thomas B. Dyett, Mrs. Carita Owens, Mrs. Daisy C. Reed, Francis E. Rivers, Eddie Johnson, Henry C. Parker, Jr., and Dr. Thomas A.

Amsterdam News Photo.
Major C. J. Peterson.

"Evening Star" [Peekskill] September 14, 1935:
Major Peterson of Peekskill on Duty at Camp Smith

Tomorrow is visiting Sunday at Camp Smith and it is expected that there will be large crowds from New York. Negro troops are stationed at the Camp this week, and will continue their practice until next Sunday, September 22nd, when the training season for 1935 comes to an end.

247

Major Clinton Peterson, a native of Peekskill, is one of the officers now at Camp Smith. He served as the first secretary of Peekskill Post of the American Legion.

In 1934, Peterson was promoted to Major, in command of the Third Battalion, the one in which he served nearly twenty years earlier. At age forty-three he was tall, strong and deeply committed to the regiment which served as the corner-stone of his life. In March 1937, he was on his way to study advanced military science at Fort Benning, Georgia, where post commandant Lt. Col. George C. Marshall had instituted revolutionary new ideas for military training (tactical improvisation combined with new concepts in mechanized/tank warfare). As the world was headed for another World War, Peterson was poised to see his old, well-tested regiment, into action once again.

369th Infantry, training in the 1930s. From "369th Infantry Regiment Photos," *Piedmont Virginia Digital History*

"Pittsburgh Courier" March 13, 1937
To Study Advanced Military Science

Group of officers of Harlem's 369th Infantry regiment, N. Y. National Guard, who left last week for the officers' training school at Camp Benning, Georgia pose with the regimental commander and his aide. The men will pursue advanced courses in military science and tactics. Left to right: Major DeMaurice Moore, Major Wilmer F. Lucas, Col. John G. Grimley Lt. Col. James M. Roche, Major Clinton J. Peterson and Captain James W. Johnson, regimental adjutant.—Courier photo by Morgan Smith, New York.

SERVICE RECORD

B-DCH-SCH-ETC	UNITED STATES	MILITIA
Peterson, Clinton J.	WW–Corp Co K 15	Pvt Co K 15 Inf . . . . .12 May 17
B–NY... 7 Jun 91	Inf. . . . . .15 Jul 17	Corp. . . . . 4 Aug 17
Den–(54)	Sgt. . . . . .12 Sep 17	A–US. . . . . 5 Aug 17
	1 Sgt . . . . .12 Sep 18	Pvt Co K 369 Inf . . . . .10 Jul 23
	HD . . . . .22 Feb 19	Trfd Hq Co. . . . . 9 Dec 23
	AEF. . . . . .14 Dec 17	Stf Sgt. . . . . 9 Dec 23
	to . . . . 9 Feb 19	2 Lt 369 Inf (A) . . . . 1 Apr 24
		Trfd Co D . . . . .21 Aug 24
		1 Lt (G) . . . . .15 Jul 25
		Trfd Co E. . . . . 4 May 26
		Trfd Co A. . . . . 1 Apr 27
		Trfd Co C . . . . 1 Jul 27
		Capt 369 Inf (C). . . . . . . 19 Oct 27
		Maj 369 Inf (Hq 3 Bn). . . . 2 Jan 34
		Trfd ING . . . . 1 Dec 37
		HD. . . . . 2 Mar 39

FULL NAME (LAST NAME, FIRST)

PETERSON, CLINTON JEROME

Service record of Clinton J. Peterson,
Honorably Discharged March 2, 1939:

Captain Peterson, with medals, including the Croix de Guerre   EFHS

250

By 1940, the Petersons had moved into a new home in Jamaica, Queens, at 111-12 177th Street. He was still employed as a postal clerk, but Olga was no longer working. Joining the couple was Olga's father, Edward Graham, native of Louisiana, aged sixty-six and retired. The neighborhood was predominantly white however there were a number of black families residing there. It had been a long journey from the Putnam County Almshouse to suburban Queens.

In 1938, Colonel Benjamin O. Davis, the first African American commander of the 369th, was appointed head of the regiment, with Lt. Colonel Chauncey M. Hooper as second-in-command. The regiment was reorganized as a Coast Artillery unit and would see service in the Pacific during World War II. On November 8, 1940, Governor Lehman of New York promoted Lieut. Col. Chauncey M. Hooper of New York City to command of the 369th Coast Artillery, colored regiment of the New York National Guard. He and Clinton J. Peterson had been early volunteers in the Old 15th, and both served with distinction as sergeants in the trenches of France as young men. In a letter from Col. Hooper dated December 1943, he addresses his old comrade with the affectionate nickname, "Pete."

Hooper to Peterson, WW II letter.   EFHS

251

At home, life was tinged with difficulty. Major Peterson's health was declining, as may be seen by comparing his youthful, full face in 1919 with the gaunt visage of the 1930s. In addition, Olga was no longer employed by the railroad mail service. As a result of the Great Depression, spouses were not permitted to jointly work with the same service and she was let go. For ten years, Olga strived in vain to be allowed back to work there, but her case was rebuffed, even though Clinton was no longer working there due to ill health. Finally, in 1943, she did secure a position in the US Postal Service on an interim basis because of the shortage of mail postal clerks. The following letter from old family friend, Congressman Hamilton Fish, demonstrates the degree to which she tried to get back to her old position, where she had first met her husband.

ILTON FISH
qn Dist, New York

COMMITTEE
Rules
Foreign Aff

Congress of the United States
House of Representatives
Washington, D. C.

March 22, 1939.

Mrs. Olga Peterson,
111-12 177th St.,
St. Albans, New York.

Dear Mrs. Peterson:

Replying to your letter, I believe it would be best if you would write me the details of the matter you have which you wish to take up with me, as it is so uncertain when I will be in New York again and when I am there I am so tied up with matters of urgent importance, that I think I could handle whatever you had in mind by correspondence better than through a personal interview.

In any event I would require the facts in writing, so that I could take whatever it is up with the proper department, and assure you that I will do whatever I can to help you and your husband.

Assuring you of my cooperation, I am,

Sincerely yours,

Hamilton Fish

In 1942, with America at war, the government undertook what was known as the Old Man's Draft Registration, targeting men born between 1877 and 1897. Peterson was listed, although ill-health had forced his retirement from the regiment on March 2, 1939. Only fifty years old, his illness kept him from work. He and Olga were still living in Queens, and their lives together had been enjoyable, with outings to Coney Island and social events with the regiment. But time was running out for our subject. Whether it was the effects of poison gas from the Great War, in combination with smoking, his health had been on the decline.

REGISTRATION CARD—(Men born on or after April 28, 1877 and on or before February 16, 1897)

SERIAL NUMBER — u 673 — NAME (Print) Clinton Jerome Peterson — ORDER NUMBER

2. PLACE OF RESIDENCE (Print) 111-12 177 St. Jamaica Queens N.Y.
(Number and street) (Town, township, village or city) (County) (State)

[THE PLACE OF RESIDENCE GIVEN ON THE LINE ABOVE WILL DETERMINE LOCAL BOARD JURISDICTION; LINE 2 OF REGISTRATION CERTIFICATE WILL BE IDENTICAL]

3. MAILING ADDRESS Same
[Mailing address if other than place indicated on line 2. If same insert word same]

4. TELEPHONE Ja 6-4668

5. AGE IN YEARS 50

DATE OF BIRTH June 7 1891

6. PLACE OF BIRTH Carmel, New York.
(Town or county) (State)

7. NAME AND ADDRESS OF PERSON WHO WILL ALWAYS KNOW YOUR ADDRESS Olga W. Peterson,

8. EMPLOYER'S NAME AND ADDRESS None

9. PLACE OF EMPLOYMENT OR BUSINESS

(Number and street or R. F. D. number) (Town) (County) (State)

I AFFIRM THAT I HAVE VERIFIED ABOVE ANSWERS AND THAT THEY ARE TRUE.

D. S. S. Form 1
(Revised 4-1-42)   (over)   16—21630-2

(Registrant's Signature)

253

Major Peterson His gaunt appearance tells of his
final illness which ended his life at age 54.   EFHS

Appendix Five
Death and Burial

"Putnam County Republican" August 24, 1945
Obituary

Major Clinton J. Peterson, who resided at Kent Cliffs thirty years ago and served in the famed 369th Infantry throughout the first World War, died at his home in St. Albans, L.I., on July 4, 1945, according to the word received here today. Military funeral services were held on July 8th, in the 15th Regiment Armory.

The following account of the services is copied from a New York paper:

Following services, conducted by the Regiment's chaplain, Captain John Bryan, assisted by former chaplains of the 369th Infantry, Captain Alexander Garner and Chaplain B.C. Robeson; and Rev. Routte, of St. Albans, the body lay in state until interment on Monday in Pinelawn National Cemetery.

The honorary pall bearers were formerly colleagues of the late Major Peterson: Col. W. Woodruff Chisum, Lt. Col. Ira Aldridge, Lt. Col. Vernon Reddick, Major Leon Brown, Captains N. Adams, John McDonald, [Dr. Thorton H.]Wood, Rufus Atkins, and Lt. Herbert Wilkie.

Major Peterson had been in ill health for some time. He began his military career on May 12, 1917, serving with the Regiment throughout the first World War. When he returned to the Regiment in 1924 and resumed his activities, he was a second lieutenant. For the next three years he served as first lieutenant and then captain. In 1927 he was commissioned as major and commanded the Third Battalion of the 369th Infantry until ill health caused his retirement.

The deceased was born on June 7, 1891 in Peekskill, N.Y. He attended Yorktown High School.

He is survived by his widow, Mrs. Olga Peterson, and other relatives.

The cortege was escorted from the Turner Funeral Home on West 136th street, to the Armory by personnel of the 15th Regiment headed by Major Howard C. Bates, and the Regimental Band.

As for Olga, she remarried to George L. Cuzzens of Hopewell Junction by 1949. Like Clinton and Olga, he was also an employee of the railroad mail service. They lived at a time in the Dunbar Apartments, but were back in East Fishkill, NY by 1962. George died in 1981 at age 90. They resided at 754 Rte. 376 in East Fishkill, and she passed in a nearby nursing home in 1994 at the age of 95. Peterson's papers were acquired by a local historian and given to the East Fishkill Historical Society.

Major Peterson is at rest at the Long Island National Cemetery, New York with his rank as Sergeant from his service during World War One.

Requiescat in pace Sergeant Peterson.